HOMEOWNER'S INSPECTION CHECKLIST

Prepared for CMHC by:

Ted Kesik
Ryerson Polytechnic University
Toronto (Ontario)

The project manager was Darrel R. Smith

CMHC offers a wide range of housing-related information. For details, call 1 800 668-2642
or visit our home page at **www.cmhc.ca**.

Cette publication est aussi disponible en français sous le titre : Guide d'inspection pour le propriétaire-occupant (62115).

CANADIAN CATALOGUING IN PUBLICATION DATA

Kesik, Ted (Theodore Jonathon), 1954-

Homeowner's inspection checklist

Issued also in French under title:

Guide d'inspection pour le propriétaire-occupant.

ISBN 978-0-660-18236-X

Cat. no. NH15-365/2000E

1. Dwellings—Maintenance and repair.
2. Dwellings—Remodelling.
3. Housing and health.
4. Dwellings—Energy Consumption.
I. Canada Mortgage and Housing Corporation.
II. Title.

TH4817.3K47 2000   643'.7   C00-980342-4

Revised 2002, 2007

Printed: 2004, 2006, 2007, 2008

Printed in Canada

Produced by CMHC

TABLE OF CONTENTS

KEEP YOUR HOME HEALTHY!

KEEP YOUR HOME HEALTHY!

If you're like most Canadians, your home is probably the biggest investment you'll ever make. Good preventive maintenance, and prompt repair when required, will help you protect that investment over the long term, and help keep your home healthy, safe and sound.

The *Homeowner's Inspection Checklist* will help you identify symptoms, cause and cures for common problems in homes. This book is not a comprehensive inspection manual, nor will it replace an examination by a qualified home inspector. It *will* help you determine if you need a thorough inspection, if you can repair a problem yourself, or if you should consult a professional tradesperson or contractor.

The *Homeowner's Inspection Checklist* will also help you assess how a home measures up according to the principles of Homeowner's occupant health, energy efficiency, conservation of resources, environmental impact and affordability. This will help you determine the steps you can take to improve and maintain the health and environmental performance of a home.

Before you buy

If you are thinking of buying an existing home, you can use this book to conduct a preliminary investigation, and decide if you want to hire a qualified home inspector to look at everything with a more trained and experienced eye. One good guideline is to hire an inspector who has no personal stake in finding trouble— he or she should not work for a roofer, or a plumber or a renovation contractor. An independent home inspection company or a licensed professional engineer who specializes in home inspections can give you the best evaluation and list of priorities for what should be done.

If you are planning to buy a house, the best advice is to carefully consider the cost of estimated repairs and maintenance. When improvement costs are added to the purchase price, you may find that the house costs too much. (Ask your real estate agent or mortgage lender about CMHC's Purchase Plus Improvements Mortgage Insurance.) Improvements may also boost the value of the house beyond the value of other houses in the neighbourhood.

Before you renovate

Good preventive maintenance is usually easy to do yourself and can prevent major repairs. If you determine that repairs are required, or there are improvements you would like to make, the *Homeowner's Inspection Checklist* can help you decide whether to do-it-yourself, hire a repair person, a professional renovator or other housing specialist.

Homeowners must consider many important factors when planning home improvements. Budgeting for the work is a major factor in most households. It is just as important to plan renovations carefully so they create as little upheaval as possible in your family's day-to-day life. Before doing any maintenance or repair, you will want to check your provincial or territorial building code and municipal bylaws, as well as insurance and liability requirements. If you do the work yourself, follow good safety practices, and always

Homeowner's Inspection

The keys to a thorough inspection are:

- being well-organized
- having your paperwork in order
- following a logical procedure

Remember:

- wear suitable clothing
- be sure you have a flashlight
- take a camera with a flash to record things you want to show an expert
- use binoculars to inspect the roof and flashings—they're safer than climbing a ladder
- inspect during the day
- allow at least two hours for an inspection

follow product manufacturer's instructions and maintenance requirements.

CMHC recommends professional assistance for major or complex projects. In this case, you should always ensure you have a written contract. Don't be tempted by the "underground operator" who offers you a discount for a cash "deal". These transactions are risky, and could leave you unprotected, with no legal recourse if the job goes wrong. Ask family and friends for names of legitimate contractors, and contact your local home builders' association or municipal building department for a list of professional renovators in your area.

Keep it up!

Homeowners don't usually inspect their houses systematically. Yet with automobiles, inspection and preventive maintenance are things that we do without even thinking. We check to see that the tires are not flat before driving. We constantly monitor fluid levels and motor condition. We check the oil, water level and wiper fluid regularly and in a systematic manner we have the whole car inspected and tuned-up. We are constantly watching for problems. Some of them we can take care of ourselves. Others, we leave to qualified auto mechanics.

A home needs a lot of tender loving care. Some homeowners forget that, and tend to let problems go until they demand attention, or become non-functional, uncomfortable or sometimes, even dangerous.

The *Homeowner's Inspection Checklist* will help you keep your entire house in top shape, all the time, with the least effort and the least expense.

About this book

There are five suggested steps to follow when you use Homeowner's Inspection Checklist:

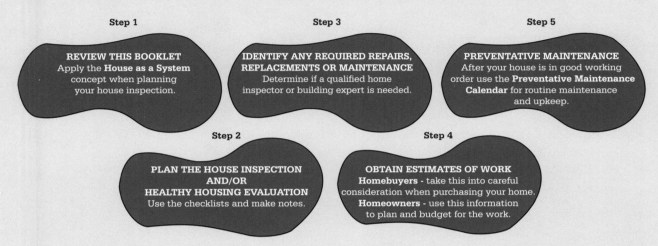

Step 1

REVIEW THIS BOOKLET
Apply the **House as a System** concept when planning your house inspection.

Step 3

IDENTIFY ANY REQUIRED REPAIRS, REPLACEMENTS OR MAINTENANCE
Determine if a qualified home inspector or building expert is needed.

Step 5

PREVENTATIVE MAINTENANCE
After your house is in good working order use the **Preventative Maintenance Calendar** for routine maintenance and upkeep.

Step 2

PLAN THE HOUSE INSPECTION AND/OR HEALTHY HOUSING EVALUATION
Use the checklists and make notes.

Step 4

OBTAIN ESTIMATES OF WORK
Homebuyers - take this into careful consideration when purchasing your home.
Homeowners - use this information to plan and budget for the work.

The following sections of the book will guide you through the process. The "House as a system" will help you understand how the components involved in your home interact with each other. The next sections focus on particular areas of the house—**basements, living areas, attics and roofs**, and **exterior walls**—and on specific areas of concern—**condensation, termites and other pests**, and **security**. Each of these sections describe common problems and offer solutions. For each of these a recommended source to consult is provided, along with the estimated skill level required to carry out the maintenance or repair:

Skill level 1: Simple maintenance

Skill level 2: Handy homeowner/homebuyer

Skill level 3: Skilled homeowner/homebuyer

Skill level 4: Qualified tradesperson/contractor

Skill level 5: Specialist/Expert

Lists of CMHC publications that you can consult for more information on specific subjects are included at the end of each section.

The Homeowner's Evaluation Tool will help you assess the environmental performance of your home balancing occupant health, energy efficiency, conservation of resources, environmental impact and affordability.

The Maintenance Calendar at the end of this book is a weekly guide to routine tasks. Everything is listed at its proper maintenance time so you won't forget anything during the year. Whole house maintenance is much less intimidating when you spread it out over a year in easy, small tasks.

CHAPTER TWO

THE HOUSE AS A SYSTEM

THE "HOUSE AS A SYSTEM"

Most people are aware that a house consists of a foundation, walls, windows and doors, which are covered by a roof, and serviced with electricity, plumbing and heating. The style of the house, its location, the layout of rooms and the quality of features and finishes are important to homebuyers and homeowners alike. Equally important, but much less obvious, is the fitness of the house. Fitness has less to do with the condition of individual components, but more with the overall condition and performance of the "house as a system".

The "house as a system" concept is an important tool. It enables building professionals to quickly assess the fitness of a house. Think of your house as a system. The concept is easy to understand and apply, and will give you with a better understanding of how a house works.

"House as a system" components

Every system is made up of components and subsystems, which interact with one another. The "house as a system" is made up of four components:

Building envelope—the foundations, floors, walls, windows, doors and roof. They enclose the house, separating it from the outdoors and protecting it from the weather.

Mechanical systems—heating, air-conditioning and ventilation systems. They control indoor air quality, temperature and relative humidity, which affect the comfort and health of the occupants of the house.

Occupants—the people, pets and plants living in the house. They interact with the building envelope and mechanical system.

External environment—the local weather, climate and building site. They affect the building envelope, mechanical systems and occupants.

Interaction

Three physical mechanisms interact with the components of the "house as a system":

Moisture flow—the flow of water and vapour across and within the building envelope

Heat flow—the conductive, convective and radiative flow of heat

Air flow—the air flow across and through the building envelope as a result of air leakage and ventilation

In the "house as a system", moisture flow, heat flow and air flow all take place all the

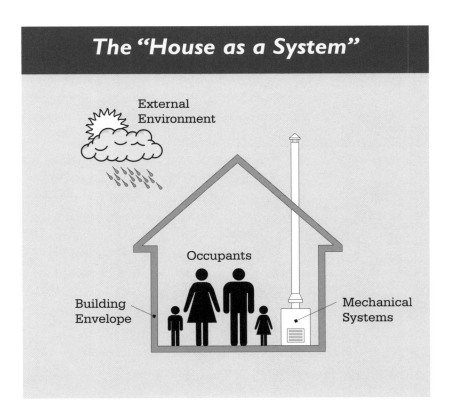

The "House as a System"

External Environment

Occupants

Building Envelope

Mechanical Systems

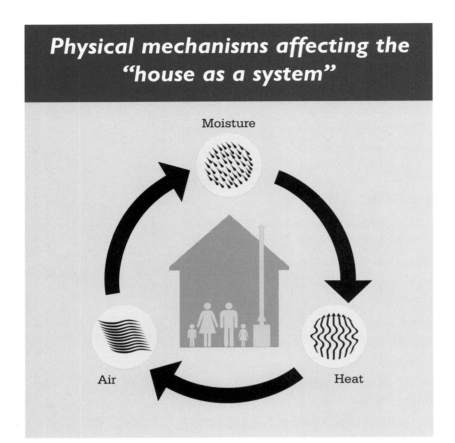

Physical mechanisms affecting the "house as a system"

Moisture

Air

Heat

energy efficiency, indoor air quality, health and safety are not compromised.

Moisture balance

In some houses the amount of moisture being generated indoors is greater than what is expelled to the outdoors. This can result from damp or leaky basements, storing large amounts of firewood indoors, or activities such as washing, cooking or bathing. In order to maintain a proper moisture balance, the excess moisture must be vented to the outside, or it may cause mold growth, comfort problems and excessive condensation on the windows. It can even lead to moisture damage of the building envelope. Many of the more serious problems in houses result from a failure to control the entry of water from the outside, and improper moisture balance, or relative humidity, inside.

Heat balance

Houses that are poorly insulated and leaky will not only lose a great deal of heat, which causes high energy bills, but also will cause occupants noticeable discomfort. Discomfort caused by an inadequate building envelope will especially affect young children and the elderly. In upgraded homes an older furnace may have too much heating capacity, causing it to rapidly cycle on and off for extended periods. The lack of continuous heat circulation may result in uneven heating of the house.

Air pressure balance

High air pressure differences in a house can lead to serious problems, such as the spillage of products of combustion from furnaces and water heaters into the dwelling.

For example, if an older, leaky house has been renovated, it will usually have been

time. In winter, heat and warm, moist air escape through leaks in the building envelope. To compensate, the furnace must supply the amount of heat being lost, and the indoor air may have to be humidified for occupant health and comfort.

The occupants of the house can exert as great an influence as the climate through their activities. This explains why a house may be very fit when one or two people occupy it, but have problems when a large, active family moves in. Problems occur when the balance of moisture, heat and air flow in the house is disturbed.

Balance

The key to the fitness of the house is the balance of the three physical mechanisms shown below so that durability, comfort, made more airtight. It is possible for large capacity air exhausting appliances such as central vacuums, clothes dryers or countertop grilles to exhaust house air at such a rate that outside air will be drawn in through chimneys and flue pipes. This can cause spillage and under some circumstances carbon monoxide (CO) poisoning. Soot deposits around flue pipes and fireplace openings, or the smoking of wood burning appliances are signs that the air pressure balance of the house is not being properly maintained.

The "House as a system" balance determines its overall fitness. Always keep this concept in mind when inspecting a house. It will make it easier to spot serious problems and to assure yourself that the house is healthy, safe and sound. The following sections of this book present detailed inspection checklists that include items pertaining to the "House as a system" balance.

CMHC Publications

The following publications offer more information on the topics described in this section. To order publications, visit our website at www.cmhc.ca or call 1-800-668-2642. The publication order numbers are shown in the brackets below.

Canadian Wood-Frame House Construction (61010)

Healthy Housing™ Renovation Planner (60957)

CHAPTER THREE

BASEMENTS

- Foundation walls
- Wall cracks
- Structural
- Heating
- Ventilation
- Electrical service and wiring
- Plumbing

BASEMENTS

Basements serve many purposes. They are a foundation for the house structure. Many services such as water, natural gas and electricity enter the house through the basement. Heating and ventilation equipment is usually installed in basements.

You can usually learn more about the condition of a house from the basement or crawlspace than anywhere else. Many problems in other parts of the house originate in the basement, making it the ideal place to begin your inspection.

Before inspecting the other areas of the house, make sure that you have covered all the items on the basement checklists. Make notes about what items need repairs, and what couldn't be inspected because it was inaccessible or not operable.

Foundation walls

Moisture coming into the basement causes most foundation wall problems. Irregularities and minor, stable cracks that do not leak water do not have to be repaired, although you may want to improve the wall as a precaution before finishing the basement. The best repairs are usually done from the outside, although some inside repairs may be adequate.

Look for...

❑ Wall cracks and water leaks

❑ Wall cracks, no leaks

❑ Efflorescence

❑ Water stains

❑ Water seepage

❑ Damp spots

❑ Crumbling mortar or concrete

❑ High moisture levels in basement or crawlspace

❑ Start the basement inspection from the outside. Walk around the house and examine the basement walls above the ground. Note any problems such as cracks or loose mortar. Check to see that the ground, walkways and driveway slope away from the foundation.

❑ Next, go inside the basement and begin the inspection with the foundation walls and then proceed according to the order in this section of the book. Remember: bring a flashlight.

❑ The condition of the foundation and main structural members in the basement is critical to the fitness of any house—be certain that these are sound and durable.

❑ Moisture, mold, and odours coming from the floor drains or sump pit are signs of an unfit basement. You must find and correct the causes.

❑ Inspect plumbing, electrical, heating and ventilation systems to make sure they are in good operating condition and to find what needs maintenance, repair or replacement.

❑ If you plan to finish the basement make sure it is dry, that the basement ceiling is high enough and that windows are suitable. Consider how plumbing, heating and ventilation will work in the finished basement—ideally, the existing systems will be suitable.

Wall cracks

Shrinkage during construction usually causes minor cracks, which are common. Settlement of the house usually causes large cracks. They can go right through the wall and tend to taper from a wide opening to a hairline crack, either from top to bottom, or from bottom to top. An old crack showing signs of getting bigger can be a sign of serious structural damage.

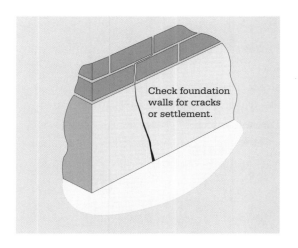

Check foundation walls for cracks or settlement.

Wall cracks			
Problem	**Cause and solution**	**Consult**	**Skill Level**
Unchanging large cracks	Fill from inside, and where possible from the outside) with "hydroscopic" concrete patch material. Hydroscopic concrete patch material expands as it dries.	Building materials supplier	3
Unchanging small cracks	Cover with "cementitious" patching material from inside.	Building materials supplier	2
Changing cracks	Consult a structural engineer or basement specialist.	Yellow Pages™	5

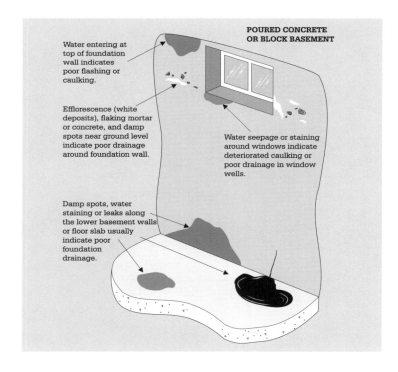

POURED CONCRETE OR BLOCK BASEMENT

Water entering at top of foundation wall indicates poor flashing or caulking.

Efflorescence (white deposits), flaking mortar or concrete, and damp spots near ground level indicate poor drainage around foundation wall.

Water seepage or staining around windows indicate deteriorated caulking or poor drainage in window wells.

Damp spots, water staining or leaks along the lower basement walls or floor slab usually indicate poor foundation drainage.

Efflorescence, Water stains, Water seepage, Damp spots, Crumbling mortar or concrete

Damp spots, crumbling and cracked mortar, or a white powdery deposit called efflorescence are signs of moisture and water seepage through the foundation. Usually, poor drainage around the outside causes the problem. If surface water causes the seepage, the seepage will usually appear near ground level, decreasing towards the floor. Ground water may appear as moisture low on the wall, or it may appear where the wall meets the floor.

Water seepage

Condition	Cause and solution	Consult	Skill Level
Water entering low down on the wall	Ground water will cause problems if the wall has not been dampproofed. Another possible cause is an overloaded or plugged drainage system—or the lack of a drainage system. This can be corrected by laying a tile drain around the basement, and dampproofing the exterior walls. Working from the exterior of the foundation is the most effective method. Because it requires excavation, it is expensive and disruptive.	Professional renovator	4
Water entering near ground level, decreasing towards the floor	Possible causes of problems from surface water include: • a downspout emptying beside the foundation wall • improper grading of the property • poor caulking around the basement windows • no drainage tile to weeping system in window wells • too little crushed stone for effective drainage Correct site drainage.	Repair as required	2
Water entering high up on the basement wall	Lack of caulking on outside of windows. Recaulk as required.	Building materials supplier	1
	Inadequate flashing under the exterior siding.	Siding contractor	4
High moisture levels in basement or crawlspace	Exposed dirt floors in basements or crawlspaces can allow large quantities of moisture to evaporate into the air. Lay a 6 mm polyethylene vapour barrier on the dirt—lap the seams and weigh them down. Protect any pathways for accessing equipment, storage areas, and so on, with boards or large diameter gravel.	Repair as required	2
Water seepage in a permanent (preserved) wood foundation	The secret of a successful preserved wood foundation is a very good drainage system that starts just under the topsoil, goes down the walls and under the foundation wall, drains completely under the floor and discharges out a sump pump or a gravity drain. Moisture problems are usually a result of a problem with the sump pump or the drain outlet. Check that the sump pump is operating properly and discharging away from the house. Check that the drain outlet is clear and running free.	Waterproofing contractor	4

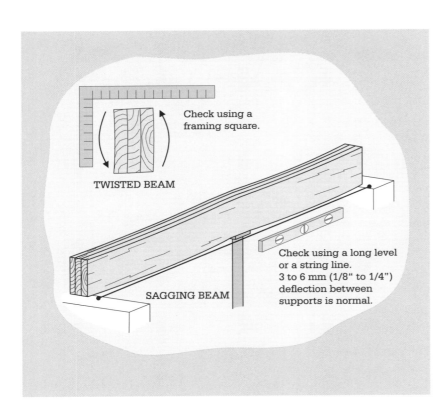

Check using a framing square.

TWISTED BEAM

SAGGING BEAM

Check using a long level or a string line. 3 to 6 mm (1/8" to 1/4") deflection between supports is normal.

Structural

Along with foundation walls, beams and columns in the basement are the main support for the house. A wall, beam or column that sags, twists or weakens will alter the structure, causing cracks in the walls, uneven floors, doors out of plumb, or sticking windows. Prompt repairs will prevent more serious problems. However, replacing or repairing defective parts is useless if the cause of the problem is not fixed. A qualified inspector, builder, renovator or engineer should inspect any condition that might suggest structural weakness.

Twisted beams			
Condition	**Cause and solution**	**Consult**	**Skill Level**
Twisted or sagging beams and floor joists	Vibrations, changes in the structure and too much weight from items such as waterbeds, hot tubs, home gyms and so on, can cause twisted or sagging beams and floor joists. Minor conditions that do not change may be acceptable. Have a structural engineer inspect any changing conditions.	Professional engineer	5
Main beam sags where a support post is located	Settlement has occurred below the post. An adjustable post may be adjusted upward to straighten the beam. Jack up a wooden timber post and install steel shim plates to level the beam.	Qualified contractor	4
	In expansive clay soils, posts may move down and back up a small distance with the seasons and continual adjustment may be necessary.	Adjust as required	2
	NOTE: Carefully monitor both of the above conditions. If settlement moves continuously downward, consult a structural engineer.	Professional engineer	5
Main beam is sagging between the supports	Either the wood is warped or the beam is over-spanned (reaching too far between supports). Add additional posts and footings, or strengthen beam.	Qualified contractor	4

Look for...

- ☐ Twisted or sagging beams
- ☐ Rotted beams or posts
- ☐ Sagging floor joists
- ☐ Mold or rot on wooden structural members
- ☐ Sinking or out-of-plumb columns

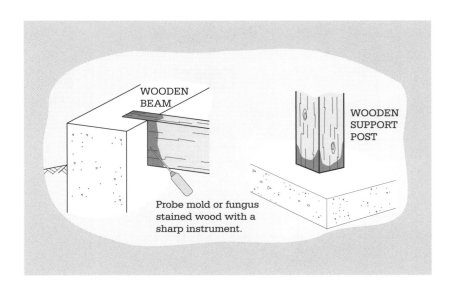

Probe mold or fungus stained wood with a sharp instrument.

WOODEN BEAM

WOODEN SUPPORT POST

Twisted or sagging beams and floor joists

Main support beams and floor joists should be square, level and true. Over long periods these structural members may slightly twist or sag. Small changes are normal. Carefully check obvious distortions.

Mold, fungus or rot in wooden structural members

Mold and rot can attack wood that stays wet for an extended period even when the indoor house temperature is normal. As the mold consumes the wood, the wood rots and loses its structural strength. For this reason, you must find and eliminate the sources of moisture causing mold growth. In many cases, mold growth on wood leaves permanent staining but no real damage. Probing the wood with a sharp object such as an ice pick will indicate if the wood is sound—it should feel as solid in affected areas as it does in unaffected areas.

Mold			
Condition	**Cause and solution**	**Consult**	**Skill Level**
Rot-deteriorated wood	Disjointed or separated parts of wooden members (delamination), and mold indicates that there might be wood decay. Probe the wood with a sharp instrument, such as an ice pick, to locate soft spots. Water leakage, poor ventilation or a lack of dampproofing—or all three—can cause wood to rot. Find the source of moisture, eliminate it, then repair or replace damaged wood. If the problem is deeper than just the surface of the wood, have a contractor replace the beam or timber post. NOTE: Termites may also cause wood to become soft or decayed, but the wood may appear unaffected on the surface. See the section of the *Checklist* entitled "Termites and Other Pests".	Qualified renovator	4

Heating

It is important to keep your heating system operating safely and efficiently. A thorough examination by a home inspector or qualified service company will show if repairs are necessary.

Look for...

❏ Unusually high fuel bills

❏ Uneven heat distribution and/or short on-off cycles

❏ Noisy furnace fan

❏ Dents, loose joints in flue pipe

❏ Corrosion on flue pipes

❏ Soot on or near flue pipes

❏ Rusty or inoperable humidifier

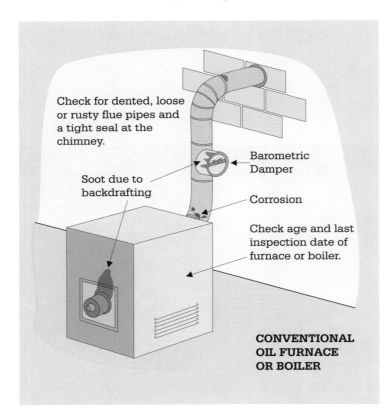

Check for dented, loose or rusty flue pipes and a tight seal at the chimney.

Soot due to backdrafting

Barometric Damper

Corrosion

Check age and last inspection date of furnace or boiler.

CONVENTIONAL OIL FURNACE OR BOILER

Oil heating

❏ Stuck barometric damper

❏ Smoky smell, oily dirt on heat registers

❏ Oil leaks

Gas and propane heating

❏ Gas odour

Electric heating

❏ Dust on heating elements

❏ Scorched drapes or furniture

Hot water and steam heating

❏ Leaks

❏ Noises during operation

❏ Uneven heating

Wood heating

❏ Creosote build-up

IMPORTANT: For all heating systems, note the date of the last inspection and information from the inspection.

A sticker giving the date and results of the last service inspection and tune-up should be on or near your furnace. Inspect oil furnaces once a year and gas furnaces once every two years. Insist on a written report showing what was inspected and tested, the test results and adjustments or repairs made. This information is useful as a record of your furnace's performance.

A high heating bill, poor heat distribution or short on-off cycles are signs the furnace needs adjusting or that there is a problem. Consult the charts for different heating systems below.

Forced-air furnace (oil, gas, electric)

Forced-air furnace (oil, gas, electric)			
Condition	**Cause and solution**	**Consult**	**Skill Level**
Dirty air filter	A dirty air filter is the most common and costly problem—costly because clogged filters can increase fuel consumption considerably. How often you have to change the filter depends on household activities and outdoor air quality. When the air filter is dirty, with plugged air holes, change the filter. Some filters can be cleaned and reused.	Manufacturer's instructions	1
Noisy furnace fan	The main cause of noisy furnace fans is a loose fan belt. Adjust the tension on the fan belt (not too tight) and tighten all loose mounting screws. Dirt on fan blades can restrict air flow and unbalance the fan. Clean carefully with a strong detergent but first turn off the electricity!	Heating contractor	4
Dents, loose joints in flue pipe	The flue pipe, which joins the furnace or boiler to the chimney, is subject to vibrations. Anything less than a well-sealed and sturdy flue pipe can reduce furnace efficiency and pose a serious fire and health hazard. Adjust, repair or replace parts immediately. Make sure there is nothing combustible within 200 mm (8 in.) of the flue pipe.	Heating contractor	4
Corrosion or rust holes on flue pipe or furnace; water marks at base of chimney	The chimney cap is cracked or missing, which allows rainwater to penetrate. Caulk, repoint or replace chimney cap.	Mason or chimney repair	4
Soot accumulation on or near flue pipe or furnace	Backdrafting brings soot, cold air and water condensation down the chimney (and deadly gases into the basement). Exhaust fans or other appliances such as the fireplace are pulling air into your house through the furnace chimney. Provide an outdoor air supply to your furnace through a controlled make-up air duct.	Heating contractor	4
Rusty or inoperable humidifier	Humidifiers attached to forced air heating systems often require more cleaning and maintenance than the furnace itself. If neglected, the humidifier will clog and corrode, and eventually stop working. Replace defective humidifier, or disconnect if no longer needed.	Heating contractor	4

Forced-air furnace (oil, gas, electric)

Oil furnaces			
Condition	Cause and solution	Consult	Skill Level
Stuck barometric damper in flue pipe	Dirt or soot can cause the damper to stick and not swing freely. Brush or scrape whatever is blocking the damper. Do not adjust the balance yourself—leave that to the service company during the annual tune-up.	Heating contractor	4
Smoky smell in the house; oily dirt around forced-air heating registers	This usually indicates a cracked heat exchanger inside the furnace. This sends some exhaust smoke into the house rather than up the chimney. This is a serious furnace problem. Contact a heating specialist immediately.	Oil heating contractor	4
Oil spillage	A faulty tank, piping or valves cause the spillage of fuel oil. A qualified oil furnace servicing company immediately should check oil spillage or even a strong smell of oil. Once the problem is solved, eliminate the odour by generously sprinkling bicarbonate of soda directly on the spilled oil, leaving it for a day, then sweeping it up. Repeat as necessary.	Oil heating contractor	4

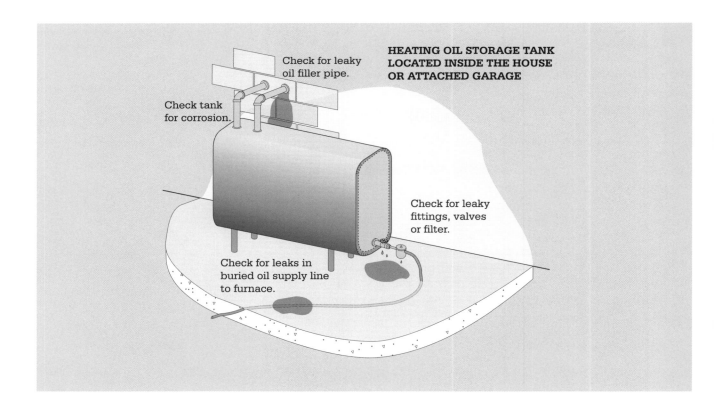

Check for leaky oil filler pipe.

HEATING OIL STORAGE TANK LOCATED INSIDE THE HOUSE OR ATTACHED GARAGE

Check tank for corrosion.

Check for leaky fittings, valves or filter.

Check for leaks in buried oil supply line to furnace.

Natural gas and propane furnaces

Gas and propane furnaces require less attention than oil furnaces because they have a "cleaner" burn. However, they can still pose a hazard.

Natural gas or propane furnaces			
Condition	**Cause and solution**	**Consult**	**Skill Level**
Gas odour	Natural gas and propane companies add a substance to natural gas and propane to give it a foul, skunk-like odour so it can be smelled if it leaks. Natural gas and propane are extremely flammable. If there is a leak • eliminate all ignition sources **immediately** • **do not smoke** • **do not use the phone (use a neighbour's phone or cell phone)** • **do not turn electrical switches on or off** • evacuate the house immediately	Notify your natural gas utility or propane gas supplier **immediately**.	5

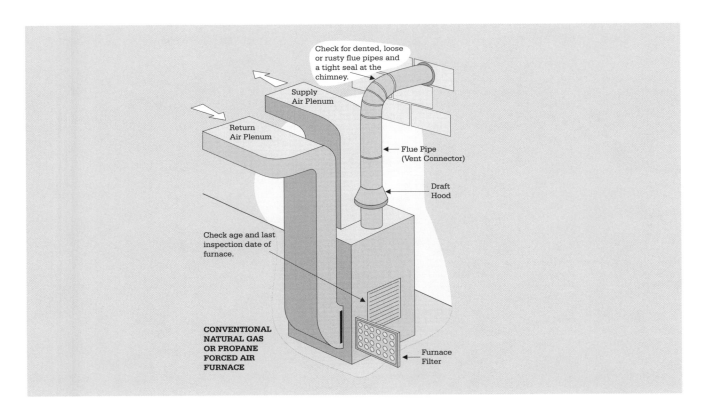

Check for dented, loose or rusty flue pipes and a tight seal at the chimney.

Supply Air Plenum

Return Air Plenum

Flue Pipe (Vent Connector)

Draft Hood

Check age and last inspection date of furnace.

CONVENTIONAL NATURAL GAS OR PROPANE FORCED AIR FURNACE

Furnace Filter

Electric baseboard heating

Electric baseboard heating			
Condition	**Cause and solution**	**Consult**	**Skill Level**
Dust on heating elements	Heating elements can pollute the air in the house as they scorch household dust with the heat. As well, dust on heating elements reduces heating efficiency. Vacuum or dust the fins on the heating elements before the heating season.	Manufacturer's instructions	1
Scorched drapes or furniture	Permanently installed furnishings or drapes that are too close to heaters can become scorched. Move the furnishing or have an electrician move or adjust the heater.	Electrical contractor	4

Hot water and steam heating

Hot water and steam heating systems are among the most durable and reliable residential heating systems. However, they can be quite old and need maintenance and adjustment.

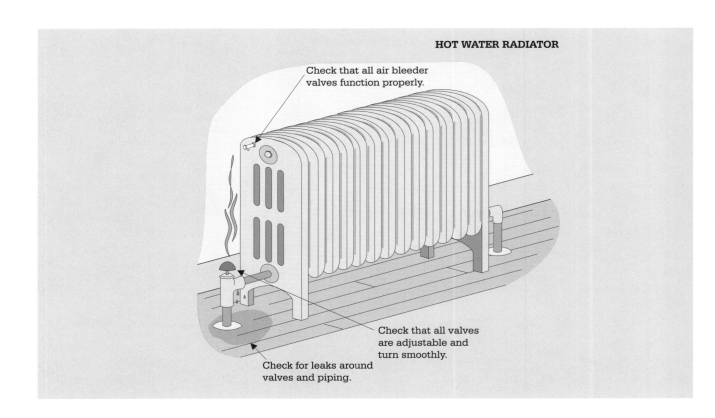

HOT WATER RADIATOR

Check that all air bleeder valves function properly.

Check that all valves are adjustable and turn smoothly.

Check for leaks around valves and piping.

Hot water and steam heating

Condition	Cause and solution	Consult	Skill Level
Noises, uneven heating	Air in the system prevents the circulation of water, causing both noises and cold radiators. "Bleed off" the air through the small valve at the top of each radiator (newer types of radiators have automatic bleeding devices which may be clogged). Bleed off all radiators at the beginning of the heating season and whenever necessary during the winter. If the problem happens often, discuss it with a heating contractor or plumber.	Manufacturer's instructions	I
Leaks	Leaks must be repaired promptly to avoid water damage. As fresh water automatically replaces the water lost by leaks, it can rust the pipes and radiators. For serious leaks, first turn off the power to the boiler, and then shut off the water supply feeding the boiler. Call a plumber or heating contractor.	Plumbing or heating contractor	4

Wood-burning appliances

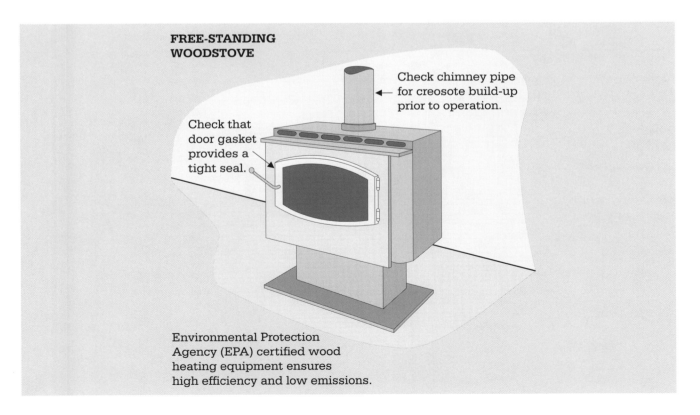

FREE-STANDING WOODSTOVE

Check chimney pipe for creosote build-up prior to operation.

Check that door gasket provides a tight seal.

Environmental Protection Agency (EPA) certified wood heating equipment ensures high efficiency and low emissions.

Wood-burning appliances

Condition	Cause and solution	Consult	Skill Level
Creosote build-up	A smouldering fire produces smoke. Smoke from a smouldering fire causes creosote build up in the chimney. Burning wet wood also causes creosote in a chimney. Excessive creosote is a serious fire hazard. Burn small hot fires, not large, slow-burning fires. Your stove may be designed to control the burn, but a furnace cannot control creosote. Clean the chimney with a suitable brush at the beginning and end of each heating season. Some chimneys will require sweeping more often. A chimney sweep or wood heating contractor can also inspect and clean your chimney.	Chimney sweep or wood-heating contractor	4
Backdrafting	Exhaust fans, clothes dryers and other appliances in the house compete with the fireplace or stove for air. When starting a fire, and when it dies down, air-exhausting appliances in the house may cause smoke to come down, not up, the chimney. Open a window when starting a fire. Provide a combustion air supply directly to wood burning appliances equipped to receive an outside air source. For other types, contact a qualified wood heating contractor.	Wood-heating contractor	4
Cracked, chipped or deteriorating firebricks inside fireplace; cracked, loose or disintegrating mortar joints	Age, abuse, excessive moisture or freeze-thaw cycles can weaken the protection of the inside lining of a fireplace. Have it checked by a wood heating specialist or a brick mason.	Wood-heating contractor or mason	4

Ventilation

Ventilation—windows that open and close, exhaust fans or a heat recovery ventilator (HRV)—is important to the health of every house and its occupants. Unless a basement is finished, it may not need mechanical ventilation, just one or two windows that can be opened and closed. Exhaust fans in basement bathrooms and kitchens are highly recommended. HRVs are usually in the basement and should be checked and properly maintained.

Look for...

❏ Stale, humid air in basement

❏ Mold or musty smell

❏ Exhaust fans either missing or ineffective

❏ HRV not working or ineffective

❏ Unvented clothes dryer

NOTE: Ventilation equipment may be in the basement, but ventilation applies to the whole house—check upper floors.

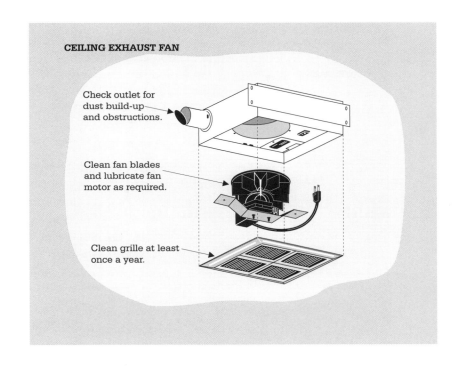

CEILING EXHAUST FAN

Check outlet for dust build-up and obstructions.

Clean fan blades and lubricate fan motor as required.

Clean grille at least once a year.

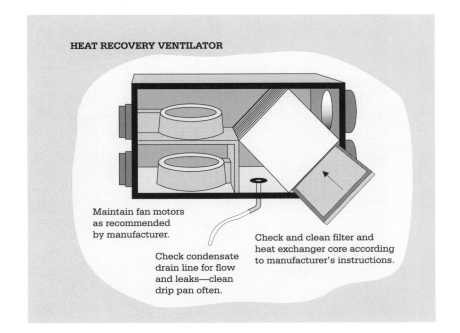

HEAT RECOVERY VENTILATOR

Maintain fan motors as recommended by manufacturer.

Check condensate drain line for flow and leaks—clean drip pan often.

Check and clean filter and heat exchanger core according to manufacturer's instructions.

Ventilation

Condition	Cause and solution	Consult	Skill Level
Stale air in basement	Poor air circulation in basements is a common problem. Most older houses were built with a cellar that was not intended as a basement living area. If the house is heated with a forced-air furnace, run the furnace fan continuously to circulate the air between the basement and upper floors.	Operate furnace fan as required	1
	In houses with electric baseboard heaters or hot water radiators, opening the basement windows and windows on upper floors from time to time (keep basement door open during this time) will flush stale air from the basement. This practice is not energy conserving in winter and not recommended during the peak summer months unless a dehumidifier is installed in the basement.	Ventilate basement as required	1
	In basements, an exhaust fan or ventilation system should be installed and operated as required.	Ventilation or heating contractor	4
Mold and musty smell in basement	Mold and mildew are more moisture-related problems than ventilation problems. If sources of moisture are not properly controlled in the basement, conditions will become ideal for mold growth. Avoid storing water-laden materials such as firewood. Drying laundry can also increase humidity levels and create conditions for mold and mildew. Install a dehumidifier to control humidity levels in the air. Place the dehumidifier in an open area and adjust it to maintain dry air in the basement. Clean it frequently.	Hardware or department store	1
	If the mold and musty smell persists after eliminating moisture sources and dehumidifying the basement, check carpeting and underlay. It may be moldy. Remove or clean affected carpeting and furnishings. Carpeting in basements is not recommended.	Carpet and furniture cleaners	2

Ventilation (cont.)

Condition	Cause and solution	Consult	Skill Level
Exhaust fan ineffective	Exhaust fans need to have clean fan blades and unrestricted, unobstructed outlets and ducts to the outdoors. Exhaust fan air flow depends on how easy it is to draw air out of a space—too tight an enclosure can virtually suffocate the fan of exhaust air flow. Check that ducts are sealed, short and as straight as possible. Clean exhaust fan and check for obstructions in the outdoor exhaust hood.	Clean and inspect the exhaust fan and hood	1
	If the exhaust fan is clean and the duct and outdoor hood are unobstructed, check the door to the room with the exhaust fan. It should have a cut along the bottom of about 25 mm (1 in.), or a louvred grill.	Undercut door or install grille in door	2
	Finally, the exhaust fan may simply not have sufficient capacity and should be replaced with a new unit.	Electrical supply or hardware store	3
Heat recovery ventilator (HRV) not working or ineffective	The operation of most HRVs is controlled by a humidistat—a thermostat-like device that senses humidity in the air. The ideal humidistat setting is between 30 per cent and 50 per cent relative humidity. If the setting is too high and the indoor relative humidity is below this level, the unit will not turn on.		
	In some cases, the control or power switch on the HRV is not turned on, or was shut off for the summer. Check the operating instructions to determine proper operation. When HRVs are hooked up with a forced air heating system, you may have to turn the furnace fan on to start the HRV. The furnace fan circulates the fresh air throughout the house using the heating system ductwork.		
	In some cases, if the condensate pan, drain line or air filter is plugged, a sensor in the HRV prevents it from running.		
	Check humidistat setting and power switches. Check that the furnace fan switch is on. Open the unit and check condensate drain and air filter.	Manufacturer's instructions	2
	If operating the HRV does not appear to control humidity or improve indoor air quality, the problem may be plugged outdoor intake and exhaust hoods. Sometimes problems may be more difficult to detect and diagnose.	Ventilation or heating contractor	4

Electrical service and wiring

To get an idea about the condition of the wiring in your house, examine the visible wiring and the electrical service panel in your basement or attic. Sometimes house wiring is only partially upgraded, with new wiring in visible areas and old knob-and-tube wiring in other areas. It is not safe to splice the two systems together. Knob-and-tube wiring that still has its insulating cover is safe if it is not disturbed. If you plan to modify a line, replace it completely with new wiring that includes a safety ground.

Label all electrical circuits at the fuse or breaker box. Turning fuses or breakers on and off while having someone test lights and outlets will identify everything on each line. Regulations about electrical work vary greatly across the country. In some areas, knowledgeable homeowners may work on electrical wiring if they obtain the proper municipal permits. For example, in Ontario and B.C. there are simplified

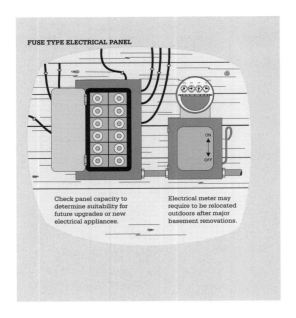

FUSE TYPE ELECTRICAL PANEL

Check panel capacity to determine suitability for future upgrades or new electrical appliances.

Electrical meter may require to be relocated outdoors after major basement renovations.

electrical code books to help people with electrical installations. In Québec and New Brunswick, only licensed electricians can legally touch the wires. However, homeowners everywhere can inspect their wiring for problems and properly manage the fuse box or circuit breakers.

Look for...

❏ Deteriorated wire insulation

❏ Exposed or bare wire

❏ Wires covered with tape

❏ Constantly blown fuses or tripped circuit breakers

❏ Lights dimming

❏ Fuses or circuit breakers which blow immediately after being reset

❏ Constantly blown main fuses or circuit breakers (insufficient capacity electrical service)

❏ Worn electrical supply lines

❏ Water leakage around electrical service entry

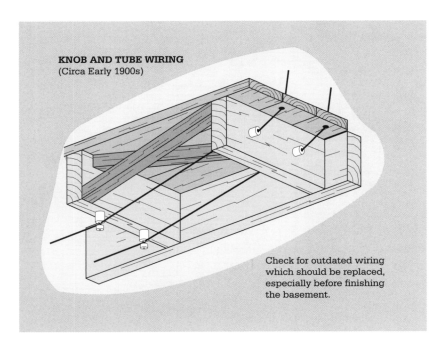

KNOB AND TUBE WIRING
(Circa Early 1900s)

Check for outdated wiring which should be replaced, especially before finishing the basement.

Electrical service and wiring

Condition	Cause and solution	Consult	Skill Level
Deteriorated wire insulation, exposed or bare wire, wires covered with tape	Age, poor workmanship or improper wire type may cause these problems. If you discover deteriorated insulation, exposed or bare wire, or even wires that were simply connected by being twisted together, have the wiring inspected by an electrician. Just because there have been no problems for the last 20 years does not mean that poor electrical connections will not cause fires in the future. Rodents may be chewing on electrical wires, in which case repairing the wiring is merely dealing with the symptoms rather than the cause. See "Rodents and small animals", later in this book.	Electrical contractor	4
Constantly blown fuses or tripped circuit breakers, lights dimming	Too many appliances are plugged into the same circuit. Older houses were not designed for modern appliances and electronic systems and few older kitchens have enough separate circuits.		
	Transfer one or more appliances to another circuit.	Electrical supply or hardware store	2
	Install a new circuit rather than use long extension cords or multiple plugs.	Electrical contractor	4
	WARNING: Do not increase the capacity of a circuit by using a larger fuse. The fuse is there to prevent wires from getting hot and causing fires. Bypassing a fuse invites trouble. Place plastic fuse "size limiters" in the fuse socket to prevent anyone from installing a larger fuse than appropriate.		
Fuses or circuit breakers blow right after being replaced or reset	There is a short circuit somewhere in the wiring circuit. Disconnect all appliances on that circuit and try a new fuse. If the new fuse blows, call an electrician to find the hidden short circuit. If it does not blow, the short circuit is in an appliance. Try them individually until you locate the problem. Also check all visible appliance wiring.	Check circuit	2
Constantly blown main fuses or circuit breakers	The electrical service is overloaded or unbalanced. This usually happens when there is a large electrical load, such as an electric range, electric clothes dryer or electric water heater operating at the same time. An electrician should rebalance or upgrade your service.	Electrical contractor	4
Worn electrical supply lines; water leakage around electrical service entry	Check the electrical service lines entering your house. Make sure the entry mast (or conduit) is secure. Check for water leakage around the mast or at the switch panel. Look for tree branches that could fall on the electrical lines. Call your local electric utility if you find any problems.	Local hydro authority	5

Plumbing

Most plumbing systems are hidden behind walls, under floors or inside cupboards. Inspect as best you can. Before inspecting plumbing, turn on each faucet, shower fixture, tub fixture and hose bib and flush all toilets. Watch them work and note the water pressure. Mark main and secondary water shut-off valves with large, visible tags that are easy to see in a plumbing emergency.

Look for...

❏ Water dripping from pipes

❏ Rust stains on galvanized steel pipes

❏ Rotting wood

❏ Low water pressure

❏ Poor drainage

❏ Gurgling noises when draining

❏ Leaking or dripping taps

❏ Leaks around toilet

❏ Condensation on toilet tank

❏ Loose toilet fixtures

❏ Hot water temperature (too hot or cold)

❏ Floor drains which give off odours

❏ Sump pump causing moisture or odour problems

❏ Water pump which will not start, or turns on too often

❏ Water pump which will not stop

❏ Scum draining through septic tank outlet device

❏ Excessive sludge in septic tank

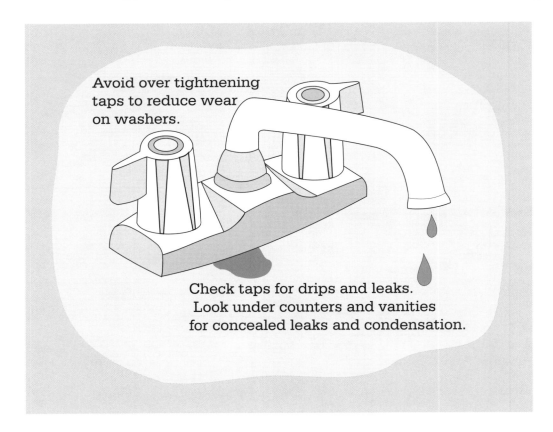

Avoid over tightnening taps to reduce wear on washers.

Check taps for drips and leaks.
Look under counters and vanities
for concealed leaks and condensation.

Plumbing

Condition	Cause and solution	Consult	Skill Level
Water dripping from pipes, rust stains on galvanized steel pipes, rotting wood	You can check for leaks in hard-to-see places by putting dry newspaper under the pipes and later checking for water drips on the paper. Sometimes leaks you think are coming from joints in the pipes are actually coming from the seam between the sink and counter top or from faulty taps and seals.		
	Condensation—Cold water running through pipes can chill the metal enough to cause moisture in the air to collect and drip as condensation. This is easily confused with a leak. If the condensation is ONLY present when it is very humid or the water is extremely cold it is probably not a leak. For condensation, reduce the humidity in the air by ventilation or dehumidification. Wrap the pipe in insulation.	Building material supplier or hardware store	1
	Leaks—Very old pipes can leak from age or mechanical abuse and will usually show rust stains at the joints. Copper piping can be poorly soldered. If hot water copper pipes touch galvanized metal (ventilation ducts or galvanized water pipes) the point of contact can quickly corrode and develop a hole. For leaks, replace very old pipes. Use rubber spacers between pipes and ventilation ducts (any rubber will do). Use "dialectal couplings" at joints between copper and galvanized pipes.	Plumbing supplier	3
Low water pressure	Low water pressure indicates problems with the water supply. Pipes or faucets may be partially plugged with rust or lime deposits.		
	Check if your neighbours have the same problem. If they do, contact your municipality about the water supply.	Neighbours, municipality	1
	If you are the only one with a problem, have a plumber check the pipes. If a pump and pressure tank is supplying water, check that these are operating properly (see Water pumps, later in this section).	Plumbing contractor	4

Plumbing (cont.)

Condition	Cause and solution	Consult	Skill Level
Poor drainage, gurgling noises when draining	You have an obstructed, poorly installed or missing vent system. Locate the vent stack (the end must be above the roof, not in the attic). Check that it is not obstructed by a bird's nest or ice accumulation. If this does not improve drainage, have a plumber inspect the system. House settlement has changed the slope of the drains. If drains are too flat, too steep, or have sags they will clog up. Plumbing straps may be able to adequately support a sagging pipe. Serious structural shifting of the house may require major replumbing of drains.	Plumbing contractor	4
Leaking taps	Worn washers. Corroded seats (what the washers push against). If changing the rubber washer does not stop the leak for long, replace the "seat" inside the faucet or replace the entire unit. In the fall, don't forget to close shut-offs for the outdoor hose bibs to prevent freezing and bursting of pipes.	Plumbing supply or hardware store	3
Leaks around toilet, loose toilet fixtures	Very cold water in frequently used toilets can cause enough condensation around the tank to rot the floor just as quickly as a real leak. Insulated toilet tanks are available to prevent this problem. Make sure the toilet is securely fastened to the floor and there are no leaks at the seal beneath the toilet. This can cause early deterioration of the floor, and unpleasant odours. Repairing the toilet before it causes the floor to rot is simple. After the floor has deteriorated, repairs are a major and expensive job. Check areas around the sink and bathtub as well for evidence of leaks and potentially rotting wood. Replace if necessary.	Plumbing supply or hardward store	3
Hot water temperature	Scalding water can cause serious injury in seconds. Excessive water temperatures also waste energy. Lukewarm water temperature is usually an indication of heavy sediment deposits at the base of the hot water tank, a faulty thermostat or electric element. For scalding water, adjust the water temperature to a maximum of 50°C (120°F). For lukewarm water, open the drain tap to see if the tank is plugged at the bottom. Attach a hose and drain sediment completely. If these solutions don't work, call a plumber or your local utility if the water heater is a rental unit.	Plumbing or heating contractor or local utility	3

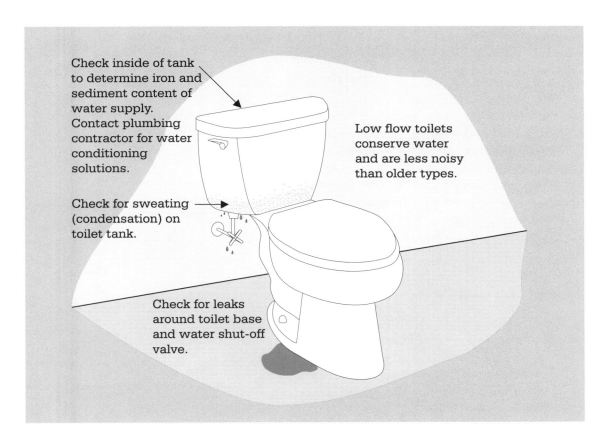

Check inside of tank to determine iron and sediment content of water supply. Contact plumbing contractor for water conditioning solutions.

Low flow toilets conserve water and are less noisy than older types.

Check for sweating (condensation) on toilet tank.

Check for leaks around toilet base and water shut-off valve.

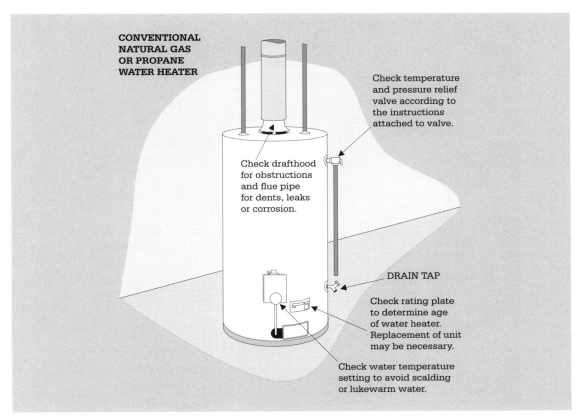

CONVENTIONAL NATURAL GAS OR PROPANE WATER HEATER

Check temperature and pressure relief valve according to the instructions attached to valve.

Check drafthood for obstructions and flue pipe for dents, leaks or corrosion.

DRAIN TAP

Check rating plate to determine age of water heater. Replacement of unit may be necessary.

Check water temperature setting to avoid scalding or lukewarm water.

Plumbing (cont.)

Condition	Cause and solution	Consult	Skill Level
Floor drains give off foul odours	Floor drains with incompletely sealed traps usually cause a smell of sewer gas in a basement. When the plug of water in the trap does not provide a complete seal, sewer gases may enter the house. Ventilate the basement, and try filling the traps with water by slowly pouring water from a pail into the floor drain or laundry tub. If this does not improve the situation, the floor drain may not have a trap (common in older homes). Replace the floor drain with a drain that has a trap.	Plumbing contractor	4
	An alternative to periodically filling the floor drains with water is to install a retrofit floor drain device which controls sewer gas.	Plumbing supplier	3
Sump pump causing moisture or odour problems	Sump pumps are used when gravity drainage by weeping tile is not possible. Aside from mechanical failure of the pump itself, two common problems are moisture and odour. Dampness and even some water leakage may occur in the basement unless an appropriate float level setting is used on a sump pump. An improperly sealed sump pit can cause odours and humidity.		
	Check the float level and make sure the switch is properly engaged when the pit starts to fill with water (use a bucket or a hose to fill the pit). Replace the switch if it does not engage when tripped. Check pump motor if the switch is not defective.	Plumbing supply or hardware store	3
	If moisture problems persist even though the pump works properly and begins to evacuate water before more than 150 mm (6 in.) accumulates at the bottom of the pit, the sump pit may have to be dug deeper, and the discharge piping extended.		
	For the control of odour and humidity, check the sump pit cover and repair or replace as required to ensure a tight-fitting seal. On the other hand, if the pump is old, replace it with a newer unit housed in a polyethylene sump pit tank that provides an airtight seal.	Plumbing contractor	4

FLOOR DRAINS

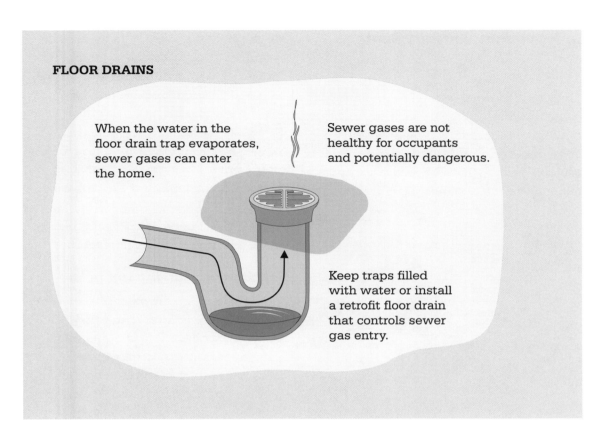

When the water in the floor drain trap evaporates, sewer gases can enter the home.

Sewer gases are not healthy for occupants and potentially dangerous.

Keep traps filled with water or install a retrofit floor drain that controls sewer gas entry.

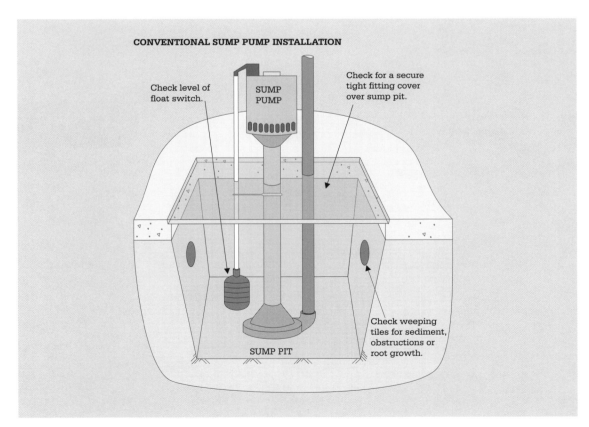

CONVENTIONAL SUMP PUMP INSTALLATION

Check level of float switch.

SUMP PUMP

Check for a secure tight fitting cover over sump pit.

Check weeping tiles for sediment, obstructions or root growth.

SUMP PIT

Independent water systems

Wells

From time to time, test well water for contamination or high concentrations of minerals. In most areas the municipal department of health will do a free bacterial analysis and give advice about maintaining safety standards. Filters in any water system, including many water treatment devices, can cause more contamination than they remove if they are not regularly cleaned and maintained.

Water pumps

Submersible jet and piston pumps are the most common pumps. They function with a pressure tank, and the tank causes most well problems. A qualified serviceperson should make major repairs to the pump or submerged pipes.

Septic tanks and disposal fields

Septic systems are the most common way to treat sewage in areas that do not have municipal services. Properly operated and maintained, septic systems can provide 20 to 30 years of trouble-free service before the field bed has to be replaced. When inspecting a home for purchase, find out how old the system is in order to estimate its remaining service life and to estimate future costs. Also check the last inspection or pump-out date.

Check tubs, sinks and toilets for rust stains—an indication of high iron content in water supply.

Soap residue in tubs and sinks is an indication of hard water.

Water conditioners for most water supply problems are available. Consult your plumber.

PRECAST CONCRETE SEPTIC TANK

Avoid inhalation of septic tank gases and any sources of ignition.

INLET

ACCESS COVERS

Avoid putting any chemicals into the septic tank—these can disrupt the sewage digestion process.

OUTLET TO FIELD BED

BOTTOM OF OUTLET

CMHC Publications

The following publications offer more information on the topics described in this section. To order publications, visit our website at www.cmhc.ca or call 1-800-668-2642. The publication order numbers are shown in the brackets below.

Investigating, Diagnosing and Treating Your Damp Basement (61065)

Healthy Housing™ Renovation Planner (60957)

Independent water systems			
Condition	**Cause and solution**	**Consult**	**Skill Level**
Contaminated well water	Clean and maintain system filters.	Manufacturer's instructions	1
	Follow advice of municipal health department.	Municipal health department	1
Soap residue in sinks and tubs, scale deposit in kettle	Hard water is the most common problem in well systems. Some household soaps will not dissolve properly in hard water and leave a residue in sinks and tubs. Hard water will also leave deposits in kettles, water heaters and pressure tanks. The deposits reduce operating efficiency. Installing a water softener usually solves the problem.	Plumbing contractor	4
Water pump will not start, pump stops, pump turns on too often	A waterlogged tank usually causes these problems. A pressure tank should be partly filled with air and partly with water. The air compresses and acts like a spring to give water pressure in the house. If there is no air pressure in the tank, the pump motor will go on and off every time the faucets in the house are used. If the tank is waterlogged, drain and refill the tank. For tanks with rubber bladders, check the air pressure and correct as required.	Check and maintain pressure tank	2
	If the tank is operating properly, the pressure switch may need adjustment or be defective. Adjust or replace as needed.	Plumbing supply or hardware store	3
Water pump will not stop	This happens when the pump has lost its prime. Homeowners using a well should be familiar with ways to prime a pump. Have a serviceperson show you how to do it.	Plumbing contractor	2
Scum draining through septic tank outlet device **Sludge more than 600 mm (2 ft.) deep**	Septic tanks need little maintenance, but they should be inspected once a year to measure the 'sludge' (settled solids) and the 'scum' (floating sewage) levels. Tanks should be cleaned when the scum level is within 75 mm (3 in.) of the bottom of the outlet device or if the depth of the sludge is more than 600 mm (2 ft.) If the tank is large enough to meet household needs, it should not require professional cleaning more than once every two or three years.	Septic system service	3

CHAPTER FOUR

LIVING AREAS

- Floors and stairs
- Interior walls
- Ceilings
- Windows and doors
- Kitchens and bathrooms

LIVING AREAS

Review the checklists for each room in your house. Remember that some of the problems you spotted in the basement may show their effects in other living areas. Also, other problems you find in these areas may be related to conditions outside the house.

☐ In older homes, springy, sagging or warped floors are common—check carefully for major structural deficiencies if any of these problems are extreme.

☐ Problems on the inside of exterior walls usually start from the outside—check from the outside for likely causes.

☐ Except for large cracks and bulges, especially on load-bearing walls, most problems with interior walls are cosmetic.

☐ Doors should open and shut properly. Some minor sticking is normal, but excessive binding indicates possible structural problems.

☐ Carefully inspect windows for signs of moisture damage or mold.

☐ Open and close every window to ensure that they work properly.

☐ Kitchens and bathrooms should be thoroughly inspected to ensure all fixtures and appliances operate properly. Look for moisture damage in floors, walls and ceilings. Check that all range hoods and exhaust fans function effectively.

Make sure your inspection of living areas covers every room, and that you have closely inspected rooms and areas such as closets. Make detailed notes of problems or defects in each room.

Floors and stairs

Look for...

☐ Springy, sagging or warped floors

☐ Squeaky floors or stair boards

☐ Damaged floor or stair boards

☐ Loose nails or boards

☐ Ripped carpeting

☐ Cracked, buckled, curled or torn floor coverings

☐ Adequate lighting on stairways; switches at top and bottom of stairs

☐ Missing or loose handrails or guards

☐ Other

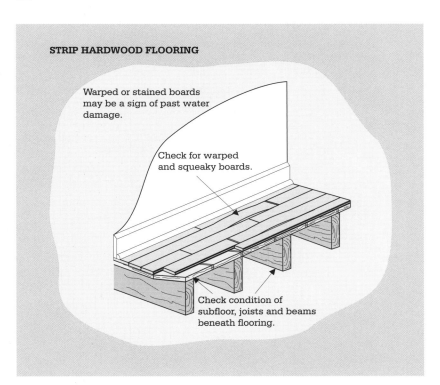

STRIP HARDWOOD FLOORING

Warped or stained boards may be a sign of past water damage.

Check for warped and squeaky boards.

Check condition of subfloor, joists and beams beneath flooring.

Floors and stairs

Condition	Cause and solution	Consult	Skill Level
Springy, sagging, and warped floors	Supports underneath are inadequate for the load. A load-bearing wall or support may have been removed from the floor below. In some cases, this results from simple settlement over time. If the problem has always been there and is unchanging it may not require correction except to make it look better. A qualified home inspector should inspect any structural movement of the house. Contact a wood flooring contractor or renovator.	Woodflooring contractor or renovator	4
Squeaking floors or stair boards	Subfloor nails that are not properly fastened to the floor joists, or inadequate shimming under the stairs at the junction of the stringers, risers or treads can result in squeaking. Squeaking floors or stairs are not serious structural or safety hazards. Fix the moving parts solidly with screws, glue or shims.	Building materials supplier	4
Damaged floor or stair boards; loose nails or boards; cracked, buckled, curled or torn floor coverings	Normal wear and tear may account for any of these problems. These problems can be serious safety hazards (such as tripping and falling). Repair them as quickly as possible.	Building materials supplier	2
Inadequate lighting for stairways	Stairways should be well lighted and have three-way light switches so lights can be turned on or off from either the top or bottom of the stairs. If the lighting on stairways is inadequate, have it improved by a qualified electrician.	Electrical contractor	4
Missing or loose handrails or guards	Stairways should have both guards and handrails for safety reasons. Loose handrails and guards often result from normal use and may have to be secured. Install proper guards and handrails if they are missing, and properly secure them if they are loose.	Stair builder or carpenter	3

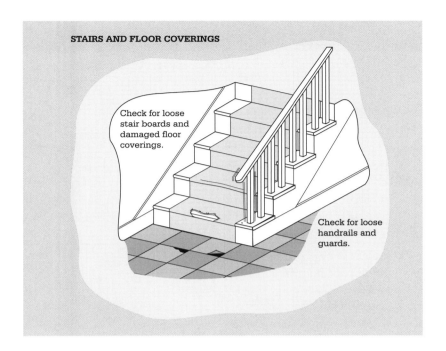

STAIRS AND FLOOR COVERINGS

Check for loose stair boards and damaged floor coverings.

Check for loose handrails and guards.

Interior walls

Interior walls in a house may be partitions between rooms, or load-bearing walls that support the floors or roof above. Outside walls are usually load bearing. A careful inspection of interior wall surfaces can tell a great deal about the condition of the house. Large cracks in plaster or drywall running diagonally over most of wall surface show serious structural problems that demand expert inspection. Lesser defects may only require cosmetic repair or minor maintenance.

Look for...

❑ Cracks or holes

❑ Unsealed joints at window frames, door frames, floor boards and countertops

❑ Bulges in plaster

❑ Faded or peeling paint and wallpaper

❑ Spongy gypsum board

❑ Mold and water stains

❑ Dusting and ghosting (wall framing)

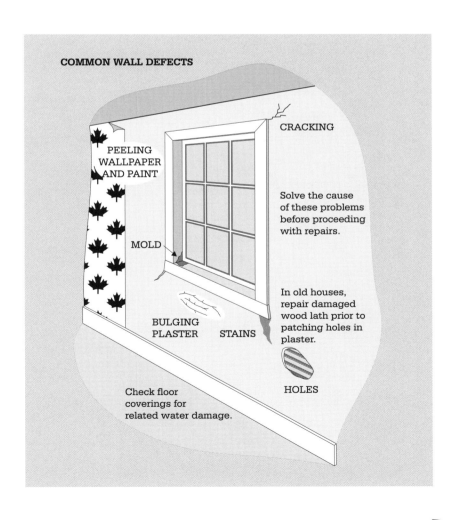

COMMON WALL DEFECTS

PEELING WALLPAPER AND PAINT

CRACKING

MOLD

Solve the cause of these problems before proceeding with repairs.

In old houses, repair damaged wood lath prior to patching holes in plaster.

BULGING PLASTER

STAINS

HOLES

Check floor coverings for related water damage.

Interior walls

Condition	Cause and solution	Consult	Skill Level
Cracks, holes, unsealed joints around window frames, door frames, floor boards and countertops	Inspect interior walls carefully—especially the interior side of exterior walls. Poor maintenance here could result in damage that is more serious. For example, rotted wood siding, peeling exterior paint and crumbling mortar may be caused by moisture leaking from inside through cracks in the walls or cracks around windows, or along the baseboard. Seal with plaster-type materials or interior caulking. Do not use exterior caulking as the solvents may be toxic.	Building materials supplier	2
Bulges in plaster	The plaster has pulled away from the lath. Tap the wall. If you hear a hollow sound, the plaster has pulled away from the lath. Tapping will also tell you how much of the plaster has pulled away from the lath. Re-plaster or cover with gypsum wallboard.	Building materials supplier	2
Faded or peeling paint and wallpaper	Age or too many coats of paint or improper painting technique (such as latex over oil paint). High moisture levels and cold walls. Strip down to a solid surface and refinish properly.	Building materials supplier	2
Spongy gypsum board, mold and water stains, dusting and ghosting of framing members	High moisture levels and cold walls are the main causes of these problems. The wall may have to be properly insulated and sealed with an air or vapour barrier.	Renovation contractor	3

Ceilings

Ceilings can indicate bulges, warps or slopes in floors above them. They may also show signs similar to those found in walls. In most cases, leaking plumbing or roofs cause the problems.

Look for...

❑ Bulging, warping, sloping and cracking

❑ Peeling paint, stains

❑ Mold growth

❑ Gaps at ceiling and wall junctions

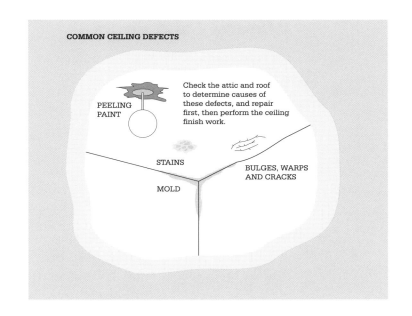

COMMON CEILING DEFECTS

PEELING PAINT

Check the attic and roof to determine causes of these defects, and repair first, then perform the ceiling finish work.

STAINS

MOLD

BULGES, WARPS AND CRACKS

Ceilings			
Condition	**Cause and solution**	**Consult**	**Skill Level**
Bulging, warps, slopes and cracks	Floors above are sagging. See Floors and stairs, earlier in this section.		
Ceilings showing problems similar to those in walls	See Interior walls on the previous page.		
Peeling paint, stains	Water seepage causes most peeling paint and stains. A roof leak is the most likely cause for ceilings under an attic or roof space. Checked during rainy weather or when snow is melting A roofing contractor can patch or replace defective roofing. Attic condensation can also cause water damage to ceilings. See the next section, Attics and Roofs. Leaking pipes, excessive moisture, or improper sealing around sinks, between bathtubs, wall tiles and floors usually causes water damage in ceilings under a living space. See Plumbing in the previous section.	Roofing contractor	3
Mold growth	Mold growth on ceilings is most common at the intersection of ceiling and exterior walls. Mold is most likely found in areas with little or no insulation and cool areas with poor air circulation, such as in closets adjacent to exterior walls. See Condensation (page 77).		
Gaps at ceiling and wall junctions	In houses with trusses, a condition known as truss uplift may cause large gaps where the walls join the ceiling. Contact a qualified home inspector or renovation contractor.	Qualified home inspector or renovator	4

Windows and doors

Windows must open to allow fresh air in and close to keep the weather out. Windows are part of the safety and security of a house, giving you an emergency exit in case of fire and locking tightly to prevent burglary. With all of these demands you must have a regular maintenance plan to keep them functioning properly.

Doors are among the very few moving parts in a house. They get the most use, wear and tear. Doors come in various styles, but they all consist essentially of the door frame, the door panel(s), and the door hardware (hinges, handles and locks). Door hardware is discussed in the Security section of this publication.

Look for...

- ❏ Stuck windows, broken glass, worn weatherstripping

- ❏ Cracked or non-existent caulking, water stains on frame and wall, rotted frame

- ❏ Excessive condensation on windows (during winter)

- ❏ Ice forming on the outside storm window or outer pane

- ❏ Ice forming inside the window

- ❏ Fogging or condensation forming between panes of glass in a sealed unit

- ❏ Door frames not square, binding or warped doors

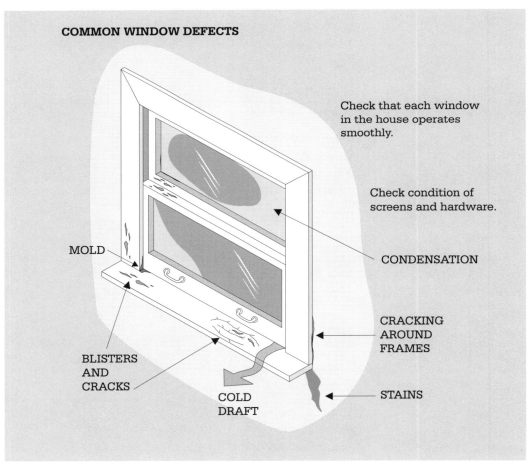

COMMON WINDOW DEFECTS

Check that each window in the house operates smoothly.

Check condition of screens and hardware.

MOLD

CONDENSATION

BLISTERS AND CRACKS

CRACKING AROUND FRAMES

COLD DRAFT

STAINS

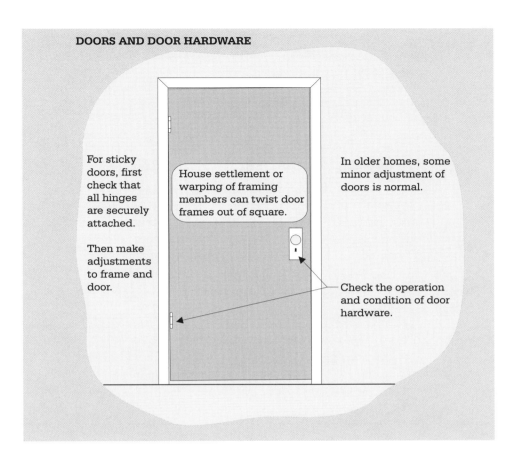

DOORS AND DOOR HARDWARE

For sticky doors, first check that all hinges are securely attached.

Then make adjustments to frame and door.

House settlement or warping of framing members can twist door frames out of square.

In older homes, some minor adjustment of doors is normal.

Check the operation and condition of door hardware.

Windows and doors			
Condition	**Cause and solution**	**Consult**	**Skill Level**
Stuck windows, broken glass, worn weatherstripping	These problems are usually caused by normal wear and tear. In extreme cases, house movement causes the problems. Clean, adjust or repair weatherstripping, and paint as necessary.	Building material supplier	2
	If windows are in extremely poor condition, have a window supplier repair or replace the windows.	Window supplier	3
	If house movement appears to be the cause of window problems, consult a qualified home inspector.	Qualified home inspector	4
Cracked or missing caulking; water stains on frame and wall	High interior humidity and poor air sealing may allow moisture in the house to seep into the wall and cause damage. Replace all damaged wall material, seal the window frame air tight to the wall on the inside of the house and lower the humidity levels in the house.	Building material supplier	2

Windows and doors (cont.)

Condition	Cause and solution	Consult	Skill Level
Excessive condensation on windows	Some condensation on windows is unavoidable, especially with single pane windows. Excessive condensation is usually caused by very poor weatherstripping on double windows, or the combination of humidity levels that are too high in the house and cold outdoor temperatures. The simplest solution is to control humidity levels with ventilation, after reducing avoidable sources of moisture in the house. Use vented range hoods when cooking and exhaust fans when bathing and showering. You may have to upgrade weatherstripping or change the window if the problem persists despite proper ventilation. In some cases, adding a plastic sheet as a third glazing layer can provide a temporary fix until your budget permits a complete solution. See also the section of this publication entitled Condensation.	Building material supplier	2
Ice forming on the outside storm window or outer pane	This is caused by warm moist air escaping past poor weatherstripping or a frame that is not sealed airtight. The moisture turns to ice on the cold pane of glass. Improve the weatherstripping or caulking on the warm side of the unit (inside the house).	Building material supplier	2
Fogging or condensation forming between panes of glass in a sealed unit	This happens when the seal on the glazing unit is defective or has failed. Have the sealed unit replaced.	Glass repair company	3
Door frames not square, binding or warped	Normal house settling may require adjustment of doors. In some cases, inadequate hinges or short screws on heavy exterior doors will not provide proper support for the door. Use spacers at the hinges, or sand or plane edges of wood doors to make minor adjustments. Seasonal temperature and humidity changes can also cause doors and frames to move. They usually only bind during the humid periods of late spring and summer. For these cases, adjust the door to work during its worst period and use weatherstripping that is flexible enough to follow the door. For wood doors, paint all edges including the top and bottom of the door slab to reduce swelling from moisture. Severe or continually changing problems may be signs of structural problems and should be inspected by a qualified home inspector.	Building material supplier Qualified home inspector	2 4

Kitchens and bathrooms

Most kitchen and bathroom problems relate to a lack of control over high moisture levels. The solutions are all basically the same; stop the creation of moisture as much as possible, reducing humidity levels by ventilating with exhaust fans and range hoods and sealing cracks that allow moisture into the walls, floors and ceiling.

Look for...

❏ No ventilation (exhaust fans or range hoods)

❏ Ventilation not functioning properly

❏ Damaged walls, ceilings or floors

❏ Rotting countertops and floors

❏ Excessive moisture, fogged windows and sweating toilets

❏ Chips and cracks on tile and grout around bathtubs or showers

❏ Damaged or missing caulking

❏ Blistering or peeling paint

❏ Soft or rotten plaster or drywall

❏ Mold on window frames or caulking beads

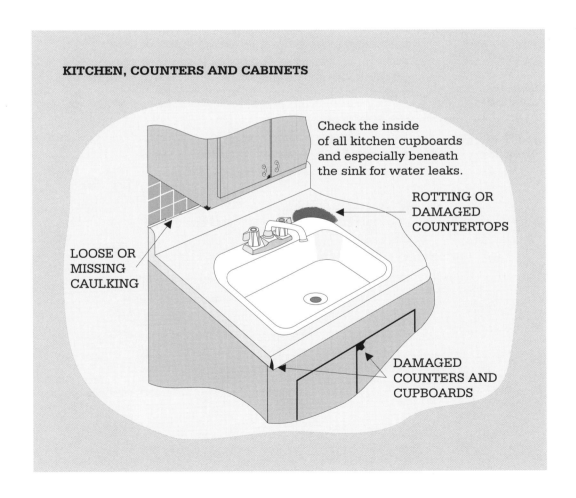

KITCHEN, COUNTERS AND CABINETS

Check the inside of all kitchen cupboards and especially beneath the sink for water leaks.

ROTTING OR DAMAGED COUNTERTOPS

LOOSE OR MISSING CAULKING

DAMAGED COUNTERS AND CUPBOARDS

Kitchens and bathrooms			
Condition	**Cause and solution**	**Consult**	**Skill Level**
No ventilation, ventilation not functioning properly	To avoid condensation problems, kitchens and bathrooms should have range hoods and exhaust fans, and the ducting and dampers must not be obstructed. Older exhaust devices may be inefficient and unable to exhaust moisture and odours properly. Install exhaust fan or range hood. Replace existing exhaust device.	Building supply or hardware store	3
Damaged walls, ceilings or floors	Moisture penetrating the framework: leaking pipes, condensation on cold pipes and toilet bowls or high humidity levels in the air. Determine the cause or causes of the moisture and eliminate it. Provide proper ventilation (See above.)	Building supply or hardware store	3
Rotting countertops and floors	Since water is likely to splash around kitchen and bathroom sinks and tubs, you should look for water seepage on the underside of countertops, the bath tub tile, the seal between the tile and tub, and also between the tub and the bathroom floor. Fix leaks, repair countertops or floors, and then provide a proper seal with caulking.	Building supply or hardware store	2
Excessive moisture, fogged windows and sweating toilets	Excessive and continual moisture, shown by wet walls, fogged windows and sweating toilets may be a sign that you are generating too much moisture or that rooms do not have enough ventilation. Opening windows may be a temporary solution (winter conditions require ventilation which cannot be addressed by opening a window), although a permanent answer is to install and operate an exhaust fan. Unlimited use of fans may cause excessive heat loss and increase your fuel bills. Control fan use with a timer or humidity-sensing switch. Bathroom doors that fit too tightly will not allow the fan to remove air from the room. Doors should be under-cut leaving an air space on the bottom or a vent grill installed to allow household air into the bathroom to allow the fan to function properly. Install exhaust fan. Replace existing exhaust device.	Building supply or hardware store	3

Kitchens and bathrooms (cont.)

Condition	Cause and solution	Consult	Skill Level
Chips and cracks on tile and grout around bathtubs or showers, damaged or missing caulking, blistering or peeling paint, soft or rotten plaster or drywall	Chips and cracks around bathtubs or showers, chipped grout or tiles and damaged caulking allow moisture to get into walls and floors. The first sign is blistering or peeling paint and soft, rotten plaster or drywall. Make repairs immediately because mold may grow, framing may rot or the exterior walls may be damaged. Repair damaged areas properly and check that the ventilation is adequate.	Building supply or hardware store	3
Mold on window frames or caulking beads	Mold is visible, usually as dark staining around windows and on caulking beads or tile grout. While bathroom cleaners can temporarily remove mold, the permanent solution is to control moisture levels with proper ventilation. In some cases, bathrooms on exterior walls may be uninsulated and become cold in winter. Cold walls tend to have condensation form on them, even when there is sufficient ventilation, and there may be mold growth. If ventilation is inadequate, install an exhaust fan or replace an existing exhaust device.	Building supply or hardware store	3
	For mold growth caused by cold exterior walls, you may have to properly insulate and air seal the exterior wall.	Qualified renovation contractor	4

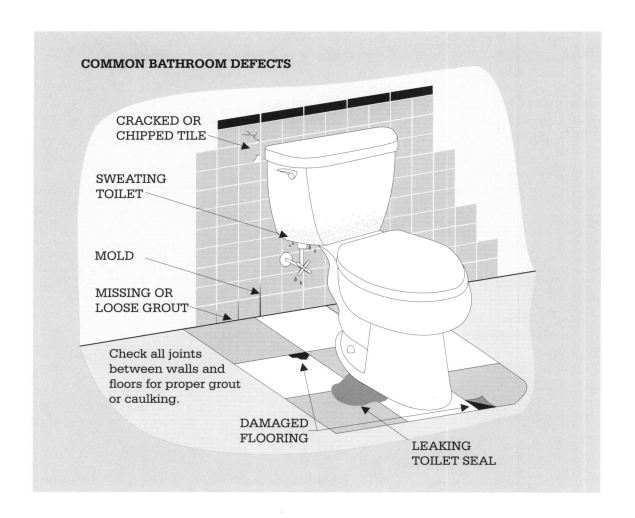

COMMON BATHROOM DEFECTS

CRACKED OR CHIPPED TILE

SWEATING TOILET

MOLD

MISSING OR LOOSE GROUT

Check all joints between walls and floors for proper grout or caulking.

DAMAGED FLOORING

LEAKING TOILET SEAL

CMHC Publications

The following publications offer more information on the topics described in this section. To order publications, visit our website at www.cmhc.ca or call 1-800-668-2642. The publication order numbers are shown in the brackets below.

Canadian Wood-Frame House Construction (61010)

Building Solutions: A Problem-Solving Guide for Builders and Renovators (60941)

Home Care: A Guide to Repair and Maintenance (61019)

Renovator's Technical Guide (61946)

Healthy Housing™ Renovation Planner (60957)

CHAPTER FIVE

ATTICS AND ROOFS

- *Attics*
- *Roofs*

ATTICS AND ROOFS

Check the attic and roof every now and then to make sure there are no problems. Small problems can turn into major damage if they are ignored. Prompt attention to problems will add years of life to your roof and attic insulation, as well as reducing the possibility of damage to the ceilings of rooms below.

❏ Inspect your attic and roof every year to avoid serious water damage in ceilings below.

❏ Replace asphalt shingles when they begin to curl and crack.

❏ Repair, refinish or preserve wood shingles. Loose wood shingles are usually a warning that the roof may soon need replacing

❏ Treat rust on metal roofs as soon as possible. Metal roofs should provide decades of durable service if they are not allowed to corrode.

❏ Check your flat roof frequently. Flat roof problems are difficult to detect, and a leak is usually the first warning of a problem. Minor repairs, such as caulking around flashing or patching a crack, are not difficult. For major problems, consult a roofing contractor.

❏ Clean eavestroughs before and after winter is important to ensure proper drainage.

❏ Check skylights, chimneys and vents for deteriorating flashing and caulking.

❏ Check chimneys for fireplaces or older heating equipment. They can have problems. In many cases, installing a metal chimney liner prevents further damage. Sometimes, the chimney will need rebuilding. Neglecting minor problems can lead to expensive repairs.

❏ Safety first. Be careful when you inspect and work in an attic or on a roof.

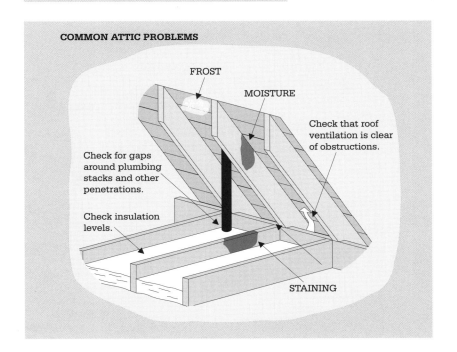

COMMON ATTIC PROBLEMS

FROST

MOISTURE

Check that roof ventilation is clear of obstructions.

Check for gaps around plumbing stacks and other penetrations.

Check insulation levels.

STAINING

Attics

Excessive moisture in the attic can weaken the roof, make insulation ineffective and damage the ceiling below. Excessive moisture can come from the roof or from indoor humidity. Sometimes it is difficult to determine just where it is coming from.

Ventilation in the roof space can help to keep an attic dry by removing humid air. It is important to provide adequate ventilation before adding insulation to the attic.

A good attic has a watertight roof and an airtight ceiling, assuring that little moisture gets in. Continuous attic ventilation from the soffits to the peak will help control moisture that accumulates in extreme conditions. (A soffit is the horizontal piece, usually wood, covering the underside of the roof overhang.)

All attics in Canada should have a minimum of 200 to 250 mm (8 to 10 in.) of insulation if room permits, without blocking the soffit vents.

Look for...

❑ Ventilation blocked by insulation or debris

❑ Wet spots

❑ Water stains on framing and roof supports

❑ Excessive dampness, moisture or humidity

❑ Water stains on the ceiling

❑ Ice dams at overhangs

❑ Frost on underside of attic roof

❑ Ducts vented into attic/roof space

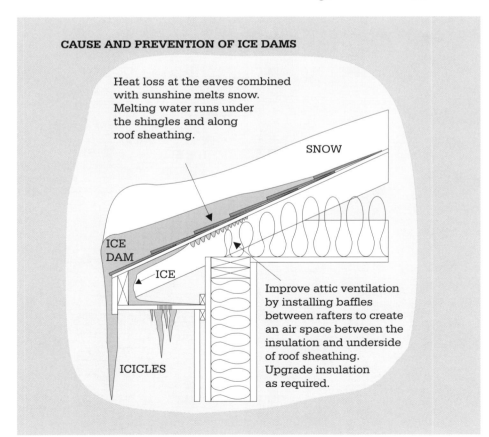

CAUSE AND PREVENTION OF ICE DAMS

Heat loss at the eaves combined with sunshine melts snow. Melting water runs under the shingles and along roof sheathing.

SNOW

ICE DAM

ICE

ICICLES

Improve attic ventilation by installing baffles between rafters to create an air space between the insulation and underside of roof sheathing. Upgrade insulation as required.

Attics

Condition	Cause and solution	Consult	Skill Level
Wet spots; water stains on framing and roof supports; excessive dampness, moisture or humidity; water stains on the ceiling	**During rainy spells:** Moisture problems during rainy spells usually mean water leakage from the roof. Most leaks come through poorly caulked flashings. See Roofs.		
	During or immediately after freezing weather: Ice dams at overhangs can result in leaks. Where house framing (outside walls, dormers) contacts the underside of a roof, heat goes through the building materials and melts the underside of the snow pack. Also, very poor attic ventilation can cause heat at the peak to melt snow. The melted snow freezes as it runs off the snow pack and creates icicles and ice dams at the lower edges of the roof. The dams back up water. The water then flows up under the shingles and into the attic.		
	Ventilate the soffits continuously so that cold air washes the entire underside of the roof on its way up to and out of vents at the peak or gables. Install insulation baffles if necessary. Make sure that all penetrations through the ceiling into the attic are sealed and make sure there is sufficient, properly and evenly installed insulation.		
	If water is leaking because of ice dams, check that the roof has eaves protection installed. If not, it should be installed as soon as possible. A roofing contractor should do the work.	Qualified roofing contractor	4
	When continuous ventilation is impossible, ice dams can be controlled with electrical heating elements, but this is an expensive solution.	Building materials supply	2
	Problems may also occur due to frost on the underside of the attic roof. Moist household air escapes into the attic and condenses or freezes. Very large quantities of water can move in this fashion—enough to make you believe that the roof leaks when warmer weather arrives. Plumbing vent stacks and exhaust ducts must not terminate in the attic and all ventilation or heating ducts that go through the attic must be insulated and sealed airtight by taping every joint.		
	Inspect the attic on a very cold day. All the moisture will be frosted and easily spotted. Air leaks are usually directly below accumulations of frost (the frost may be on the rafters, the underside of the roof or on top of the insulation). Seal off all air passageways between the house and the attic, preferably from the attic side under the insulation, or at least from inside the house. Stopping the source of the moisture problem is more important than trying to clean up the problem with ventilation. Typical problem holes are around light fixtures, fans, plumbing vent pipes, chimneys and attic entrances. Use caulking, plastic sheets and spray foam sealant.	Building materials supplier	2

Attics (cont.)

Condition	Cause and solution	Consult	Skill Level
Ventilation blocked by insulation or debris	Make sure that there are ventilation openings both low in the attic (such as eave vents or soffit vents) and high in the attic (such as ridge vents or gable vents) and that they are not blocked by the insulation, debris or by too much paint on the screens. Clean out plugged soffit vents and vacuum out debris. Install insulation baffles to provide air space between the insulation and underside of roof sheathing.	Building material supplier	2
Ducts vented into attic and roof space	In some cases, ducts or plumbing stacks are improperly vented into the attic or roof space. Correct this immediately because the moist air being vented into the attic or roof space may result in serious moisture damage. Install a proper vent hood on the roof or exterior wall and connect the open duct to the hood. The vent hood should have an insect screen and a damper. Make sure that all joints in the ducts are taped or sealed. Plumbing stacks should penetrate the roof and have a rubber flashing that is sealed to the roof covering.	Building materials supplier	3

Roofs

Examine the flashing around the chimney, vents, stacks, skylights and other areas and make sure that they are in good condition. Most roof leaks result from poor flashing or poor caulking on flashings. In older homes, check the soffit. Wooden soffits, if not properly cared for, can deteriorate quickly, letting in blowing snow, insects, rodents and birds. Replace soffits in poor condition. Note trees that could drop branches and damage the roof.

Sometimes, you can check the roof from the ground using binoculars. If there are problems and you are unfamiliar with roof repairs or cannot climb a ladder, consult an experienced contractor or qualified home inspector.

If you work on a roof:
- **never work alone**
- **never work on a wet roof**
- **never work without proper safety equipment**
- **wear shoes with good traction.**

If you feel uneasy, leave the job to a qualified contractor

Look for...

- ❏ Sagging portions of roof
- ❏ Curled and cracked shingles
- ❏ Wide spaces between shingles
- ❏ Bare patches
- ❏ Leaks
- ❏ Moss
- ❏ Curled, split, loose or rotted wood shingles
- ❏ Blisters, bare patches, curled edges or leaks on flat roof
- ❏ Corrosion of metal flashings
- ❏ Ponding on flat roofs
- ❏ Corrosion of metal roofing

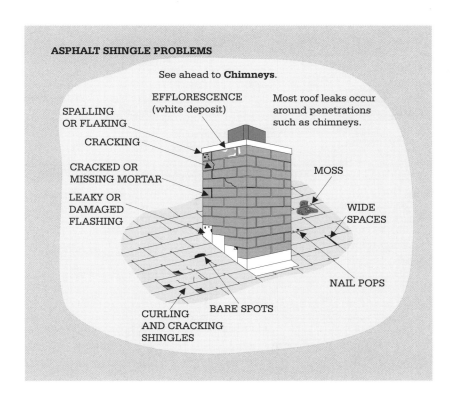

ASPHALT SHINGLE PROBLEMS

See ahead to **Chimneys**.

EFFLORESCENCE (white deposit)

Most roof leaks occur around penetrations such as chimneys.

SPALLING OR FLAKING

CRACKING

CRACKED OR MISSING MORTAR

LEAKY OR DAMAGED FLASHING

MOSS

WIDE SPACES

NAIL POPS

BARE SPOTS

CURLING AND CRACKING SHINGLES

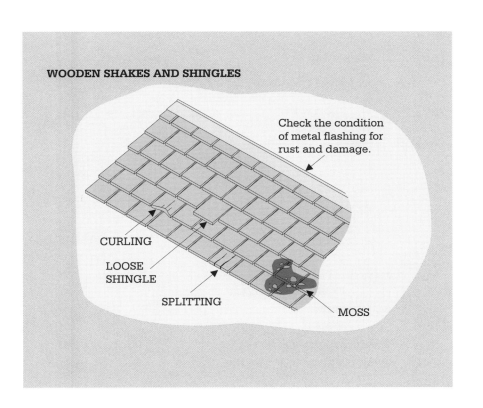

WOODEN SHAKES AND SHINGLES

Check the condition of metal flashing for rust and damage.

CURLING

LOOSE SHINGLE

SPLITTING

MOSS

Roofs

Condition	Cause and solution	Consult	Skill Level
Sagging portions of roof	Structural weakness. Consult a qualified home inspector or structural engineer to determine the cause and propose proper repair work.	Qualified home inspector or structural engineer	4
Asphalt shingles: curled and cracked, wide spaces between, bare patches, leaks	When asphalt shingles get old, they begin to shrink, curl and crack. Wind and physical abuse can also cause problems. If only a few shingles are affected, they can be repaired with roofing nails and roofing cement.	Building materials supplier	2
	If more than a few shingles are affected, you will have to reshingle the roof. Usually, new shingles can be placed directly over one layer of existing shingles for a maximum of two layers, if the base layer is flat.	Roofing contractor	4
	Holes in the flashing or lack of caulking at flashing cause most leaks. Holes from popped nails or damaged or missing shingles letting water under shingles can also cause leaks. See solutions above.	Building materials supplier	2
Built-up or flat roofing: blisters, bare patches, curled edges, leaks	All are signs that the built-up membrane is failing. The exact point of leakage can be difficult to find.		
	Small areas can be patched and repaired. NOTE: Walk as little as possible on a flat roof.	Building materials supplier	3
	A roofer specializing in flat roofs should handle re-occurring and large-scale repairs.	Roofing contractor	4
Wood shingles and shakes: curled, split, loose and/or rotted	Old wooden shingles and shakes eventually become so porous—full of tiny openings—that they can no longer keep out the rain.		
	If a few shingles or shakes are in bad condition they can be replaced or repaired.	Building materials supplier	3
	If the entire roof is in bad condition, reshingling the roof may be the best solution.	Roofing contractor	4
Moss	Moss can easily grow on roofs that are heavily shaded by trees in regions of high humidity. It is not an immediate threat to asphalt roofs although moss can shorten their life span. Metal strips and various chemicals are available to kill moss and prevent it growing again. Check with experienced users of any product to assure that it will not harm other plants.	Building materials supplier	3
	Moss promotes decay in wooden roofs because it keeps them damp. Moss should be scraped off and the affected area treated with a wood preservative.		

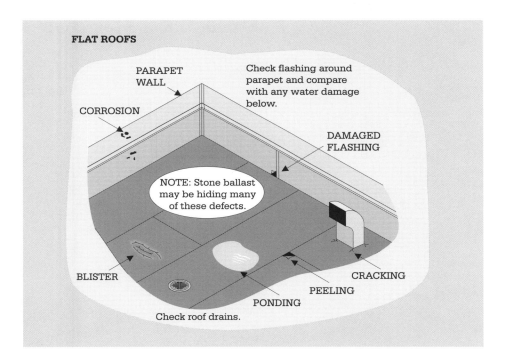

FLAT ROOFS

PARAPET WALL

CORROSION

Check flashing around parapet and compare with any water damage below.

DAMAGED FLASHING

NOTE: Stone ballast may be hiding many of these defects.

BLISTER

CRACKING

PEELING

PONDING

Check roof drains.

Roofs (cont.)			
Condition	**Cause and solution**	**Consult**	**Skill Level**
Corrosion of metal flashings	Corrosion is caused by age or physical damage.	Building materials supplier	3
	Small holes can be filled with roofing cement or strips of foil-backed mastic adhesive.		
	Badly corroded flashings should be replaced.	Roofing contractor	4
Ponding	Standing water, or 'ponding', and ice often lead to early deterioration of the roofing membrane on a built-up or flat roof. Ponding is caused by poor design, clogged drainpipes or sagging roof joists.		
	Keep wire guards on all drains. Keep drains free of leaves and other debris. Other corrective work usually involves the structure of the roof and should be done by a roofing contractor.		
Corrosion of metal roofing	Corrosion of metal roofing is caused be age, environmental or physical damage, or lack of painting maintenance.		
	Temporary repairs can be made with strips of foil-backed mastic adhesive.	Building materials supplier	3
	An experienced roofing contractor should do permanent repairs.	Roofing contractor	4

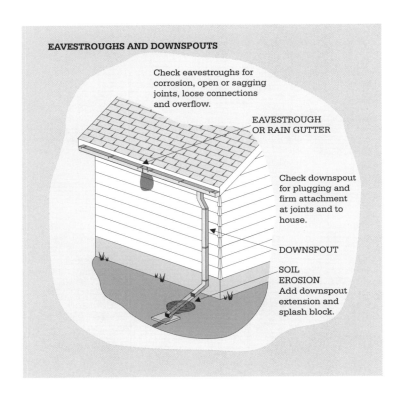

EAVESTROUGHS AND DOWNSPOUTS

Check eavestroughs for corrosion, open or sagging joints, loose connections and overflow.

EAVESTROUGH OR RAIN GUTTER

Check downspout for plugging and firm attachment at joints and to house.

DOWNSPOUT

SOIL EROSION
Add downspout extension and splash block.

Eavestroughs and downspouts

Eavestroughs and downspouts are not maintenance-free. They should be cleaned and examined at least twice a year—in the early spring and late fall.

Look for...

❑   Rust and corrosion

❑   Open joints

❑   Loose connections to house

❑   Overflowing

❑   Soil erosion below downspout

❑   Water seepage in corner of basement

❑   No downspout leaders or extensions

Eavestroughs and downspouts			
Condition	**Cause and solution**	**Consult**	**Skill Level**
Rust and corrosion, open joints, loose connections to house	Minor repairs can be made with asphalt roofing cement and should be made as soon as possible. Nails that no longer hold can be moved a couple of inches to solid wood.	Building materials supplier	2
Overflowing	Blocking from debris. Not enough slope from the trough to the downspout. Eavestroughs not lined up properly with the lip of the roof.		
	Re-install eavestrough at proper slope, plus regular maintenance.	Adjust as required	3
Downspout connected to a clogged drainage system	Clear the drain or redirect the downspout.	Adjust as required	3
Soil erosion, water seepage in corner of basement, no downspout leaders or extensions	Downspouts should direct water away from the foundation, driveway or patio. If water collects near the foundation, use a longer drainage sleeve—perhaps with holes in it—to allow the water to escape over a wider area. Or, install a downspout extension and splash block, and build up the grade to drain water away effectively.	Adjust as required	3

Chimneys

Both masonry and metal chimneys need to be straight and structurally sound, have proper capping on the top and watertight flashing where they penetrate the roof. For common defects, see Roofs.

Look for...

- ❏ Deteriorating brick
- ❏ Open mortar joints
- ❏ Leaning
- ❏ Water stains on ceiling near chimney
- ❏ No cap or deteriorating cap

CMHC Publications

The following publications offer more information on the topics described in this section. To order publications, visit our website at www.cmhc.ca or call 1-800-668-2642. The publication order numbers are shown in the brackets below.

Building Solutions: A Problem-Solving Guide for Builders and Renovators (60941)

Home Care: A Guide to Repair and Maintenance (61019)

Renovator's Technical Guide (61946)

Chimneys

Condition	Cause and solution	Consult	Skill Level
Deteriorating brick, open mortar joints, leaning	Water is getting inside the chimney structure and freeze-thaw cycles are deteriorating the bricks, the mortar or both. Make sure there is a chimney cap that prevents rainwater from settling into the mortar joints from the top. A cracked chimney cap should be caulked.	Building materials supplier	3
	A chimney should have a good inside liner of clay or metal to prevent moisture in the flue gases from saturating the bricks. Repoint open mortar joints. Consult a mason or heating specialist if you find deterioration.	Mason or heating specialist	3
	Leaning chimneys should be properly rebuilt and open mortar joints repointed.	Mason	4
Water stains on ceiling near chimney	Metal flashings joining masonry chimneys to the roof must be caulked regularly to keep them watertight. Recaulk, repair or replace flashings.	Building materials supplier	3
	Air leakage paths around chimneys that penetrate insulated roof spaces can permit moist household air into the roof area. It condenses on the side of the chimney and drips back onto the ceiling. Both metal and masonry chimneys must be flashed with fireproof material and sealed airtight at the ceiling level with high temperature caulking. Keep insulation a minimum of 50 mm (2 in.) away from the chimney.		

EXTERIOR WALLS

- Wood siding
- Metal siding
- Vinyl siding
- Brick
- Stucco

EXTERIOR WALLS

Exterior walls are built to last the life of the house. Small, outside maintenance jobs will help exterior walls last and probably save you time and money if you do them promptly. Along with improving the looks and curb appeal of a house, preventive maintenance will help stop bigger problems from developing.

All cracks that could let driving rain into the wall should be caulked with good exterior caulking materials.

- ❏ Exterior finishes provide protection from the elements as well as giving the house a pleasing appearance. Proper maintenance adds value and durability.

- ❏ Check wood siding closely to determine the condition of the paint finish—refinish before surface cracking peels.

- ❏ Metal siding needs little maintenance, but replacement is the only way to properly repair damage and defects.

- ❏ Vinyl siding can be washed to maintain a bright, clean finish. Damaged sections need to be replaced rather than repaired.

- ❏ Brick is a durable finish if maintenance and repair are done promptly. Don't just fix the symptom, deal with the cause of the problems.

- ❏ Stucco can be repaired but skill is required to blend patches with the existing stucco.

Inspect exterior walls carefully under bright light. Minor cosmetic defects are not cause for concern if they are promptly repaired Remember to note and compare exterior problems with those in living areas. They are often related and must be dealt with at the same time.

Wood siding

Wood siding is a traditional material that is durable if it is properly installed and maintained. Early detection of defects and problem areas and prompt repair and maintenance are the keys to keeping wood siding functional and pleasing.

Look for...

- ❏ Paint failure
- ❏ Splitting wood
- ❏ Dry rot
- ❏ Buckling
- ❏ Wood rotting

Too many coats of paint or too many years between paintings are the most common causes of wood siding problems. Rainwater penetrating unprotected ends, open joints or gaps also takes its toll on the finish and the wood. Moisture penetrating the siding from inside the house occurs most often on the side of the house away from prevailing wind, or the outside of rooms that generate high humidity. All of these contribute to the problems noted above.

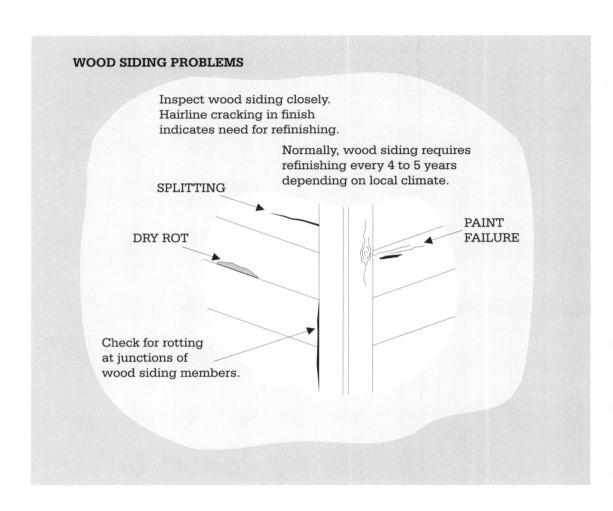

WOOD SIDING PROBLEMS

Inspect wood siding closely. Hairline cracking in finish indicates need for refinishing.

Normally, wood siding requires refinishing every 4 to 5 years depending on local climate.

SPLITTING

DRY ROT

PAINT FAILURE

Check for rotting at junctions of wood siding members.

Wood siding			
Condition	**Cause and solution**	**Consult**	**Skill Level**
Paint failure, splitting wood, dry rot, buckling	Keep siding clean, painted and sealed. Seal the wall from the inside and install adequate ventilation to reduce indoor humidity levels.	Building supply or hardware store	2
Wood rotting	Soil must not be in close contact with the siding. Re-landscape to keep siding 200 mm (8 in.) above the ground, while still avoiding water forming a pond near the foundation. Install eavestroughs with downspout extensions.	Building supply or hardware store	3

Metal siding

Metal siding is low-maintenance compared to wood, but it is not as forgiving, and quickly reveals damage or aging.

Look for...

❑ Chalked paint

❑ Pitting

❑ Corrosion

❑ Water stains under lip

❑ Dents

❑ Buckling

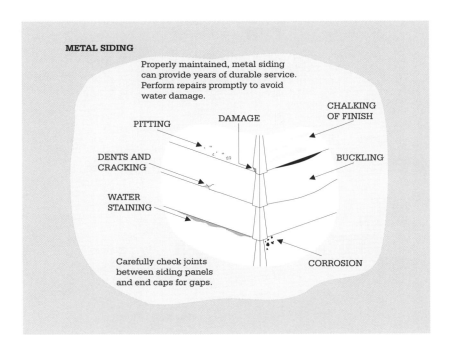

METAL SIDING

Properly maintained, metal siding can provide years of durable service. Perform repairs promptly to avoid water damage.

PITTING

DAMAGE

CHALKING OF FINISH

DENTS AND CRACKING

BUCKLING

WATER STAINING

CORROSION

Carefully check joints between siding panels and end caps for gaps.

Metal siding			
Condition	**Cause and solution**	**Consult**	**Skill Level**
Chalked paint, pitting, corrosion	Aging of the paint usually causes chalked paint although corrosion and pitting can be caused by air pollution (acid rain). Cleaning and painting will help slow deterioration. Use an all-purpose, heavy duty cleaner and follow the manufacturer's instructions. Work from the bottom up to avoid dirt streaks, then rinse from the top down.	Paint or hardware store	2
Water causes stains under lip	Water stains and moss under the lip are signs of moisture behind the siding. Check all flashings to assure no rain water is penetrating. Seal air leakage paths inside the house and ventilate rooms to prevent household moisture from penetrating through to the siding.	Building supply or hardware store	3
Dents	Hitting or leaning anything heavy against metal siding. Hail can also cause dents. Dents cannot be removed—the damaged section must be repaired with auto body filler and refinished or replaced.	Hardware store	2
Buckling	Metal siding will buckle if it is nailed too tightly. It should be free to expand and contract with temperature changes. Nails should be centred in slots and left slightly loose. This buckling action (sometimes called oil canning) produces loud noises. Removing the siding and re-applying it correctly will solve the problem.	Siding or renovation contractor	3

Vinyl siding

Vinyl siding never has to be painted and it requires cleaning only for the sake of appearance. Vinyl siding can have problems.

Look for...

❑ Chalking (from bright sunlight)

❑ Buckling

❑ Cracking

❑ Water stains under lip

Vinyl siding			
Condition	**Cause and solution**	**Consult**	**Skill Level**
Chalking	Chalking can result from bright sunlight. This cannot be repaired, but replacement of defective vinyl siding may be covered under the warranty.	Siding or renovation contractor	3
Buckling	See the discussion of buckling on the Metal siding chart, above. Vinyl siding reacts even more to temperature change than metal siding. Removing the siding and reapplying it correctly will solve buckling problems.	Siding or renovation contractor	3
Cracking	In extremely cold weather, vinyl becomes brittle. Vinyl siding is in danger of cracking if it is hit in extremely cold weather. Repair with colour-matched caulking, if it is available. If it isn't, replace the damaged section.	Building supply store	2
Water causes stains under lip	Water stains and moss under the lip are signs of moisture behind the siding. Check all flashing to assure that rain does not penetrate. Seal air leakage paths inside the house and ventilate rooms to prevent household moisture from penetrating through to the siding.	Building supply or hardware store	2

Brick

Brick veneer is a durable finish that should not be allowed to deteriorate.

Look for...

- ☐ Dirty bricks
- ☐ Crumbling mortar joints
- ☐ Cracked or loose brick
- ☐ Efflorescence (white powdery deposit)
- ☐ Moisture penetration from inside house
- ☐ Chimney brick deterioration
- ☐ Spalling or flaking of brick

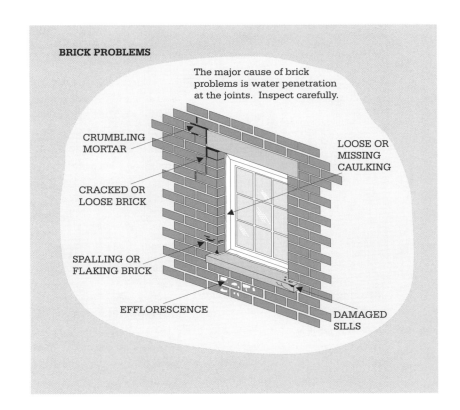

BRICK PROBLEMS

The major cause of brick problems is water penetration at the joints. Inspect carefully.

CRUMBLING MORTAR

CRACKED OR LOOSE BRICK

SPALLING OR FLAKING BRICK

EFFLORESCENCE

LOOSE OR MISSING CAULKING

DAMAGED SILLS

Brick			
Condition	**Cause and solution**	**Consult**	**Skill Level**
Dirty bricks	Atmospheric pollution, and your own chimney, can soil bricks. Never sandblast bricks: it destroys them. Bricks can be cleaned by high-pressure steam. It is best not to paint bricks. Use sealants cautiously. Bricks do not need to be waterproofed: the air space between the bricks and the house keeps them dry.	Building restoration or masonry contractor	4
Crumbling mortar	Air pollution usually causes crumbling mortar. Much of this pollution comes from the chimney. The bottom of a wall, underneath windowsills, and the top of the chimney are usually the first places that the problem appears. Improper flashing, caulking or loose mortar allows water to penetrate bricks, creating more problems. Scrape out and repoint the mortar and if necessary repair or replace bricks. Chimneys should have a concrete or metal chimney cap to protect the upper layer of bricks.	Masonry contractor	3
Cracked or loose bricks	Usually caused by settlement in the foundation. If minor, replace or repair the bricks.	Masonry contractor	3
	If extensive damage occurs, consult an engineer to check for foundation problems.	Professional engineer	5

Brick (cont.)

Condition	Cause and solution	Consult	Skill Level
Efflorescence	Efflorescence is a white powder that forms on bricks where water has penetrated and then evaporated. It is not usually a serious problem, but is a sign of moisture problems that should be dealt with. A faulty downspout or overflowing eavestrough causing continuous water flow on the brick may cause efflorescence. Interior moisture because of air leakage or high humidity levels may also be a cause. Repair the rain gutters (eavestroughs) if they are the cause. Seal air leakage paths inside the house and ventilate rooms to prevent household moisture from penetrating through to the brick veneer.	Building supply or hardware store	2
Moisture penetrating brick from inside the house	Sometimes moisture from inside the house can penetrate the brick. It does not cause efflorescence, but shows up as crumbling brick or mortar. Check that the air or vapour barrier is effective. Seal air leakage paths inside the house and ventilate rooms to prevent household moisture from penetrating through to the siding. Also make sure that the weepholes are not plugged or ineffective.	Building supply or hardware store	2
Acidic flue gases or condensation inside the chimney causing chimney brick deterioration	Have a certified metal liner installed.	Chimney repair or heating contractor	4
Spalling or flaking bricks	Spalling is breaking off or peeling of the surface layer of a brick. It is generally caused by water penetrating the brick and then freezing. The original cause is probably inferior bricks combined with poor construction. The only solution is to find why water is penetrating and then replace the bricks.	Masonry contractor	4

Stucco

Stucco is a traditional exterior finish. It depends on proper installation and control of moisture to last for a long time. Structural movement will also cause cracking.

Look for...

❏ Cracks

❏ Chips

❏ Loose or damaged areas

CMHC Publications

The following publications offer more information on the topics described in this section. To order publications, visit our website at www.cmhc.ca or call 1-800-668-2642. The publication order numbers are shown in the brackets below.

Healthy Housing™ *Renovation Planner* (60957)

Canadian Wood-Frame House Construction (61010)

Renovator's Technical Guide (61946)

Stucco			
Condition	**Cause and solution**	**Consult**	**Skill Level**
Cracks	Usually caused by frame movement of the structure behind the stucco. If the crack is growing, consult a qualified home inspector to find why the frame is moving. Solve the problem, then seal or repair the crack.	Stucco contractor	3
Chips, loose or damaged areas	Signs that water is getting behind the stucco. Water penetrating the cracks can rot the wall framing. If the water freezes it will loosen large areas of stucco. Loose stucco can be detected by tapping the wall and listening for a hollow sound. These areas should be broken off and replaced. Painting can restore small cracks and blemishes.	Stucco contractor	3

CHAPTER SEVEN

CONDENSATION

- *Surface condensation*
- *Concealed condensation*

CONDENSATION

As a result of improved energy efficiency in housing, condensation is becoming a common problem. Cooking, washing, laundering and even breathing can cause high humidity and result in condensation. Sealing your house up tightly is a good idea both to save energy and prevent condensation from forming in the walls and attic. But the house must be adequately ventilated as the sealed gaps no longer provide air movement. Open windows occasionally, use exhaust fans when necessary or install a controlled ventilation system with heat recovery system to ensure year-round economy and comfort.

❑ Most condensation problems in basements occur during the summer months. Avoid opening basement windows during hot, humid weather and use a dehumidifier to control basement moisture levels.

❑ Avoid venting clothes dryers to the indoors. Don't use kits that exhaust clothes dryer air into your house. They introduce both moisture and chemicals to indoor air.
Use exhaust fans when bathing and vented range hoods when cooking. When washing floors, shampooing carpets or painting, open a window slightly and operate exhaust fans until moisture and odours disappear.

❑ Ventilation and dehumidification can eliminate most normal levels of condensation if they work properly and you use them when needed. Avoid excessive humidity levels.

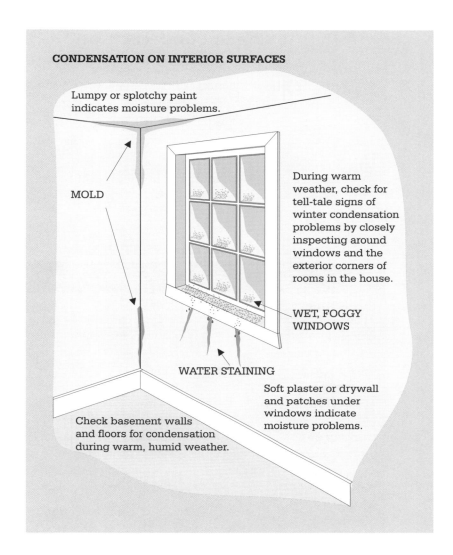

CONDENSATION ON INTERIOR SURFACES

Lumpy or splotchy paint indicates moisture problems.

MOLD

During warm weather, check for tell-tale signs of winter condensation problems by closely inspecting around windows and the exterior corners of rooms in the house.

WET, FOGGY WINDOWS

WATER STAINING

Soft plaster or drywall and patches under windows indicate moisture problems.

Check basement walls and floors for condensation during warm, humid weather.

Misty windows and damp spots on walls and ceilings are signs of high humidity and lack of insulation. Check the moisture level carefully, not allowing it to reach a point where moisture or ice build-up can occur. Otherwise, serious structural damage can be the result and repairs may be necessary.

Condensation can and should be controlled in houses. See the section of this publication entitled Basements, and check the operation of ventilation equipment and basement dehumidifiers.

Surface condensation

Surface condensation is caused by indoor humidity contacting cool surfaces. In most cases, proper ventilation will eliminate condensation. Sometimes it is necessary to seal gaps and install additional insulation. Excessive humidity and surface condensation in a house is unhealthy.

Look for...

❑ Condensation on windows

❑ Damp spots on walls, ceilings or closets

❑ Moisture on light fixtures, cold water pipes, toilets, walls and basement floors

❑ Ice appearing on windows or window frames

❑ Frost on door knobs

❑ Frozen hinges and doors

Surface condensation			
Condition	**Cause and solution**	**Consult**	**Skill Level**
Condensation on windows; damp spots on walls, ceilings or in closets; moisture on light fixtures, cold water pipes, toilets, walls and basement floors	Condensation is always caused by a combination of cold temperatures and high humidity. The colder it gets outside, the lower the humidity must be in the house to prevent condensation. Better insulated walls and windows keep inside surfaces warmer, allowing higher humidity levels in the house without condensation when it is cold outside. Sources of humidity include bathing, showering, dishwashing, laundering, cooking, houseplants, storing firewood and drying clothes inside the house. Unvented clothes dryers and gas appliances can also be sources of excess humidity.		
	You can reduce surface condensation by reducing household humidity levels: shutting off your furnace humidifier, installing exhaust fans in the bathrooms and kitchen, opening windows, venting appliances outdoors, opening drapes and curtains during the day and not hanging laundry in the house. Whole house ventilation with heat recovery is the best way to control humidity.	See also, Ventilation	1
Ice appearing on windows or window frames, frost on doorknobs, frozen hinges and doors	Ice forms when there is a combination of cold temperatures and high humidity. Ice shows that there is too much humidity in the house and that the window, door or doorknob is colder than it should be. Causes include poor design, poor installation allowing cold air in through cracks, or poor weatherstripping allowing outside air in and causing very cold surfaces.		
	Insulate between window frames and the wall and between door frames and the wall behind the trim. Seal all cracks with either caulking or weatherstripping. Improve the insulation quality of poor windows by adding storm windows on the outside, or a plastic film inside.	Building supply or hardware store	3
	Replace window units that repairs do not fix.	Window contractor	4

Concealed condensation

Concealed condensation occurs when moist air from inside the house leaks into spaces between the walls or into attics and crawl spaces. During the winter the moisture in the air freezes. When it melts you will notice dripping water or water stains. This usually appears during warm spells immediately following very cold spells. Mold may even appear.

Concealed condensation is more difficult to fix than surface condensation, and potentially more harmful to your health. The smell or sight of mold is a strong sign of concealed condensation. Deal with it immediately.

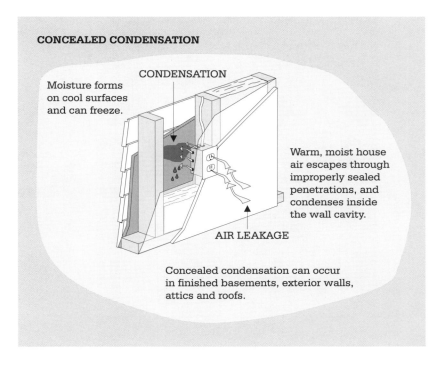

CONCEALED CONDENSATION

CONDENSATION

Moisture forms on cool surfaces and can freeze.

Warm, moist house air escapes through improperly sealed penetrations, and condenses inside the wall cavity.

AIR LEAKAGE

Concealed condensation can occur in finished basements, exterior walls, attics and roofs.

Look for...

❑ Water dripping from the ceiling

❑ Wet drywall under windows

❑ Mold coming through wall paint

❑ Dry rot

Concealed condensation			
Condition	**Cause and solution**	**Consult**	**Skill Level**
Water dripping from the ceiling, wet drywall under windows, mold coming through wall paint	Keep humidity down by controlling the sources of household humidity and providing ventilation. Disinfect all mold properly.	Building supply or hardware store	1
	Seal all electrical outlets and vents that are on exterior walls and ceilings.		2
	Seal window and door frames to the wall.		2
	Install exhaust fans or replace ineffective units.		3
	Make sure your attic has adequate ventilation and insulation.	Qualified contractor	4
	If all else fails have a home inspector find the problem.	Home inspector	4

CMHC Publications

The following publications offer more information on the topics described in this section. To order publications, visit our website at www.cmhc.ca or call 1-800-668-2642. The publication order numbers are shown in the brackets below.

About Your House: Measuring Humidity in Your Home (62027)

About Your House: Fighting Mold – The Homeowner's Guide (60516)

Clean-up Procedures for Mold in House (61091)

CHAPTER EIGHT

TERMITES AND OTHER PESTS

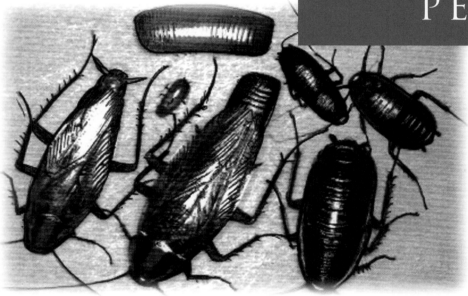

- Termites
- Other insects
- Rodents and small animals

TERMITES AND OTHER PESTS

Termites, cockroaches, rodents and other pests are not only a nuisance and potential health hazard, they can also cause serious damage to your home. Periodically check for their presence.

❑ Termites are a serious threat to the structural soundness of your house. Get professional help if you detect termites.

❑ Insects are attracted to nesting places caused by cracks and gaps—caulk and seal the exterior of the house.

❑ Rodents are attracted to food and shelter. Keep garbage under control and seal all paths leading from the outside indoors.

❑ Birds, bats and squirrels will nest in attics and under eaves. Ensure attics are sealed from unwanted intruders.

Check for termites and other pests seasonally. Inspect the outside of the house closely for openings or gaps, and seal them properly. Early detection and early blocking of entry points are the most effective means of controlling termites and other pests.

Termites

Termites are becoming more prevalent in many areas of Canada. They look like ants with long, white wings and are sometimes called "flying ants."

Look for...

❑ Sawdust

❑ Runways and tunnels in wood

❑ Mud tunnels on outside of house

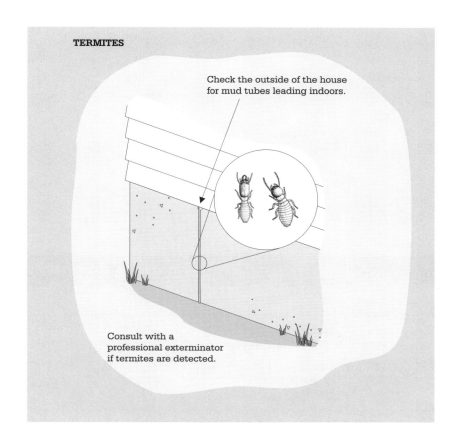

TERMITES

Check the outside of the house for mud tubes leading indoors.

Consult with a professional exterminator if termites are detected.

Other insects

Fleas, cockroaches, earwigs, silverfish and other insect pests are usually found around accumulations of garbage, in cupboards and in closets.

Look for...

❑ Fleas

❑ Cockroaches

❑ Earwigs

❑ Silverfish

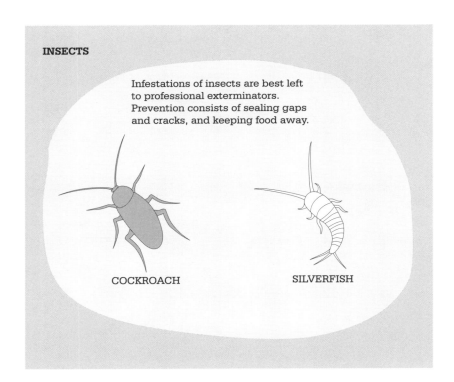

INSECTS

Infestations of insects are best left to professional exterminators. Prevention consists of sealing gaps and cracks, and keeping food away.

COCKROACH   SILVERFISH

Rodents and small animals

Look for...

❑ Holes

❑ Frayed insulation

❑ Bare wires

❑ Toothmarks on pipes or leaking pipes

CMHC Publication

Farewell to Cockroaches: Getting Rid of Cockroaches the Least Toxic Way (60948)

Termites and other pests			
Condition	**Cause and solution**	**Consult**	**Skill Level**
Sawdust, runways and tunnels in wood, mud tunnels on outside of house	Sawdust around infested wood and runways or tunnels over the surface of wood may be evidence of termites. If you suspect their presence, probe structural beams with a sharp instrument. Infested wood will be spongy or almost hollow. Call an exterminator.	Pest control company	4
Fleas, cockroaches, earwigs, silverfish	Clean up all sources of moisture and food, then fumigate. If the problem persists, call an exterminator.	Pest control company	4
Holes, frayed insulation, bare wires, toothmarks on pipes or leaking pipes	These signs may indicate the existence of small animals or rodents. Rats, mice, squirrels and other small animals can damage the framework, wiring and parts of the plumbing of a house. Birds and bats have also been known to cause damage in attics.		
	Try to seal or screen any points of entry into the house, and destroy any nests you find. WARNING: Some feces, such as those from bats, may be toxic or a source of serious infections—consult a professional or your local health unit for proper precautions.	Pest control company or municipal health authority	2
	If the problem is persistent, call a professional exterminator or municipal authorities for advice.	Pest control company	4

CHAPTER NINE

SECURITY

- *Landscaping and yard layout*
- *Security lighting*
- *Windows and doors*
- *Smoke alarms*
- *Security sensors and systems*

SECURITY

Total security that gives completely protection from professional thieves is impractical, but most break and enters are committed by individuals who look for easy prey. A properly equipped house, preventive maintenance and common sense are reasonable security from common burglary. If you are not easy prey, thieves will try somewhere else.

CMHC's booklet *How to Lock Out Crime: Protecting Your Home Against Burglary* has more-detailed information about improving your home's security.

❏ Landscaping can conceal burglars around entry points such as basement windows. Trim back or relocate shrubs and bushes for security.

❏ Windows and doors are the most common break-in points. Ensure proper hardware is installed, and use the locking devices.

❏ Lighting both outside and inside the house can be an effective deterrent. Most hardware stores sell affordable security lighting with motion alarms or timer switches.

❏ Smoke alarms save lives. Locate at least one smoke alarm on each floor, and test them periodically to ensure they function properly.

❏ Security systems are available and recommended as a second line of defense against burglary.

Security at home is something most of us take for granted until we become victims of crime. When inspecting any house, identify all of the weak points in security, and address these as soon as practically possible. Prepare your home and your family to make security part of your lifestyle.

Landscaping and yard layout

Landscaping and yard layout may not have considered home security, especially in older houses. In some cases the landscaping may be improved, but in others, vulnerable areas need more appropriate security.

Consider these questions when you assess your house landscape and yard layout:

❏ Does the fencing in your backyard safely protect young children without giving trespassers a hiding place?

❏ Do trees, shrubs or bushes conceal potential break-and-entry points in the house?

❏ Does a deck, a gazebo or other feature offer hiding places for trespassers?

Look for...

❏ Solid fencing that hides trespassers

❏ Shrubs and bushes concealing potential entry points

❏ Yard layout giving trespassers hiding places

❏ Security lighting

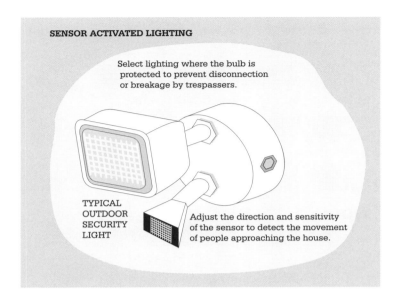

SENSOR ACTIVATED LIGHTING

Select lighting where the bulb is protected to prevent disconnection or breakage by trespassers.

TYPICAL OUTDOOR SECURITY LIGHT

Adjust the direction and sensitivity of the sensor to detect the movement of people approaching the house.

Security lighting

The same lighting that homeowners use for safety and convenience can also be security lighting when proper fixtures and controls are selected.

Look for...

- ❏ House not visible by neighbours or from street
- ❏ Lights above outside doors
- ❏ Outdoor light fixtures do not protect light bulb from removal
- ❏ Motion sensitive lights for concealed areas
- ❏ Timer or photo cell controls for house lighting

Windows and doors

When inspecting the windows and doors of the house, consider the following questions:

- ❏ Can window catches and door locks resist the moderate use of force? Are they in good shape?
- ❏ Is it easy to break glass panels in entranceways and reach in to unlock the door?
- ❏ Are all windows, doors and garages equally protected? The best front door does little good when there is an easily forced basement window nearby.
- ❏ Does a ladder or garage roof give easy access to unprotected second storey windows?
- ❏ Do you have secondary security catches so windows can be left slightly open for ventilation while remaining securely locked?

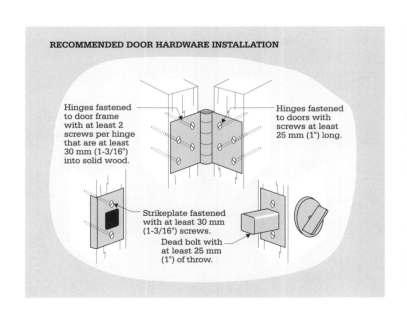

RECOMMENDED DOOR HARDWARE INSTALLATION

Hinges fastened to door frame with at least 2 screws per hinge that are at least 30 mm (1-3/16") into solid wood.

Hinges fastened to doors with screws at least 25 mm (1") long.

Strikeplate fastened with at least 30 mm (1-3/16") screws.

Dead bolt with at least 25 mm (1") of throw.

Look for...

❏ Weak locks, hinges and frames

❏ Locks on windows

❏ Viewers for exterior doors

❏ Glass area within reach of door lock

❏ Patio door rail blocking

Smoke alarms

Look for...

❏ Smoke alarms

❏ Smoke alarms improperly located

❏ Smoke alarms do not function

❏ Dead batteries

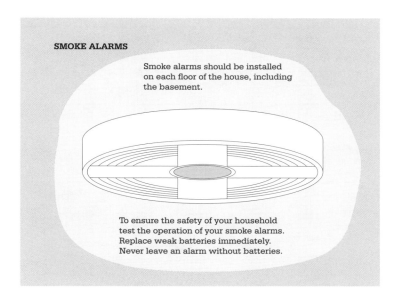

SMOKE ALARMS

Smoke alarms should be installed on each floor of the house, including the basement.

To ensure the safety of your household test the operation of your smoke alarms. Replace weak batteries immediately. Never leave an alarm without batteries.

Security sensors and systems

There are many types of security sensors or detectors available today. Some are highly specialized and detect unsafe levels of carbon monoxide, natural gas or propane. Others entire home security systems connected by telephone to emergency services. All of these are only as good as the operation and maintenance habits of the residents.

Look for...

❏ No carbon monoxide sensor

❏ Security system not working

❏ Security system disconnected

CMHC Publications

The following publications offer more information on the topics described in this section. To order publications, visit our website at www.cmhc.ca or call 1-800-668-2642. The publication order numbers are shown in the brackets below.

How to Lock Out Crime: Protecting Your Home Against Burglary (61124)

Security

Condition	Cause and solution	Consult	Skill Level
Landscaping and yard layout not secure	The key to successfully landscaping for security is to provide as few—preferably no—opportunities for concealed break and entry.		2
Inadequate security lighting	With the wide availability and selection of lighting products and controls, improving security lighting is easy and affordable. Most lighting shops and hardware stores will provide the appropriate products and assistance.	Building supply or hardware store	3
Windows and doors not secure	Review deficiencies and make a plan for improvements.	Locksmith or home security professional	4
Inadequate smoke alarms	Every house should have one or more smoke alarms. Test them to see that they are operating. Open them and vacuum or dust the inner parts once a year to prevent dust and insects from making them work. Replace batteries at the intervals as recommended by manufacturer.	Building supply or hardware store	2
No carbon monoxide sensor	Houses with wood stoves or fireplaces, or older types of natural gas, propane or oil heating equipment should have a carbon monoxide sensor. Carbon monoxide alarms are available in most electrical and hardware stores.	Building supply or hardware store	2
Security system not working or disconnected	Home security systems should be checked to ensure proper operation. In some cases, the security system alarms will be triggered, but the alarm is not forwarded by telephone signals to emergency services. Check that your existing system is functional and properly connected by periodically contacting your service company.	Security alarm services	4

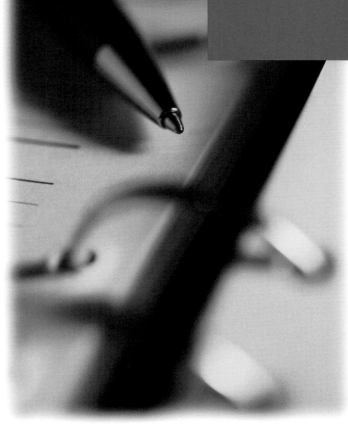

CHAPTER TEN

HOMEOWNER'S™ EVALUATION TOOL

HOMEOWNER'S EVALUATION TOOL

CMHC research in Homeowner's has helped identify the choices that can lead to housing that is better for occupants, better for the environment, and that makes good economic sense. Homeowner's provides a healthy indoor environment, uses resources such as water and energy efficiently, and is affordable. Homeowner's also responds to evolving household needs.

Why is Homeowner's important? On average, Canadians spend about 90 per cent of their time indoors, much of it at home. So it is important for us to have homes with healthy indoor environments. We must also begin to make the impact of our homes and communities on the environment as gentle as possible. Housing is a major consumer of energy and water, and a major generator of waste during construction and occupancy. Clearly, the health of the environment affects our living conditions, our social well-being and even our individual health.

❏ Homeowner's is good for its occupants, their community and the environment.

❏ The health of any home can be improved, adding real value and enhancing the quality of life for the occupants.

❏ This evaluation tool is a guide to identifying important features of a house which contribute to, or detract from, its health.

The Homeowner's evaluation tool presented in this section will help you identify the features of housing that

balances five important priorities— occupant health; energy efficency; conservation of resources; environmental impact; and affordability.

❏ **occupant health**—better indoor air quality; adaptable, accessible design

❏ **energy efficiency**—efficient building envelope, mechanical equipment, lighting and appliances, use of alternate energy technologies such as solar

❏ **conservation of resources**—durable and recycled building materials, water-conserving fixtures and appliances, resource-efficient landscaping

❏ **environmental impact**—efficient use of land; transportation patterns that contribute to reduced greenhouse gas emissions

❏ **affordability**—lower operating costs, convertible designs

How to use the Homeowner's evaluation tool

In order to get the most from the Homeowner's evaluation tool, it is important to understand clearly the meaning of the following terms.

Unfit—A condition which should be addressed immediately.

Fit—Acceptable condition with some improvement possible.

Healthy—Good condition which meets the aims of Homeowner's.

The following charts will help you evaluate the health of the home you live in or the house you are thinking of buying.

The Basement

Basements are valuable space in a house, accounting for one-half to one-third of the total floor area. Many basements are not healthy because of poorly maintained equipment or occupant lifestyle. A healthy basement can offer high quality, affordable living space and maximize the use of a house.

Unfit	Fit	Healthy
wet, damp or cold basement	dry basement	warm, dry basement
mold and musty odour/staining—no ventilation	no mold or musty smell—exhaust fan(s)	dehumidifier and ventilation system serving basement
sewer gas or fuel oil smell	no foul odours or leaking fuel lines	fresh, bright basement
paints/chemicals stored in basement	closed storage cabinet for paints and chemicals	vented or outdoor storage facility
open sump pit without cover	sump pit with cover	sump pit with seals and secure cover
soot or corrosion around furnace or water heater flue pipe	flue pipes and vents in good condition—no signs of soot	direct vent (sealed combustion) appliances
firewood stored in basement	no storage of wet or moldy materials	clean, livable basement
fuse-type electrical panel and/or knob-and-tube wiring	circuit breaker type electrical panel and grounded wiring	GFI protected circuits, block heater outlet timer
contaminated water supply, failing septic system	acceptable water and sewage disposal	reverse osmosis water filters
costly or inefficient heating	mid-efficiency gas, oil, or propane furnace and water heater	high-efficiency furnace and water heater or integrated appliance
no insulation or moisture barrier	minimal insulation and moisture barrier	full-height insulation and moisture barrier

Living areas

People spend most of their time at home in the living areas. Indoor air quality, daylight and comfort make for better occupant health. Energy efficient lighting and appliances conserve energy. Even the size and layout of rooms influence the use of housing resources.

Unfit	Fit	Healthy
rooms too small for intended use—poor layout/ circulation	adequate room sizes and ample circulation	compact but efficient house plan
evidence of mold growth	no mold	washable water-resistant finishes and mechanical ventilation
soot staining around fireplace or wood stove	properly operating wood heating equipment	CSA/EPA certified wood heating equipment and insulated chimney
floor finishes and adhesives with high content of volatile organic compounds	clean carpeting and vinyl flooring	durable floor finishes, e.g. wood, ceramic, stone/slate, vinyl composition tiles or linoleum flooring
poor daylighting because of too small or too few windows	minimum window areas provided as set in building code	ample window areas for daylighting, passive solar heating
windows painted shut, no screens, not able to ventilate the room(s)	windows with proper operating hardware and screens	windows arranged for high and low and cross-ventilation of house
no proper outdoor garbage storage facility	garbage bin or storage area	composter and recycling facility
attached garage not well sealed from house and without door closer	attached garage with carbon-monoxide alarm	detached or well-sealed garage or carport
poorly maintained appliances (no EnerGuide rating)	EnerGuide rated appliances in good condition	good EnerGuide rated and energy conserving appliances
poor-condition or leaky plumbing fixtures	good-condition plumbing fixtures	water-conserving plumbing fixtures and appliances
poor lighting	lighting in good condition	high-efficiency lighting (compact fluorescent bulbs) with timers
no ventilation	exhaust fans in bathrooms, vented range hood in kitchen	whole house ventilation system with heat recovery
no humidifier	furnace humidifier (cleaned and maintained)	stand-alone humidifier

Exterior walls

Exterior walls include windows and doors, and account for one-quarter to one-third of the heating energy used in a typical house. Exterior finishes that are damaged or failing can cause serious degradation of the house, and lead to replacements that consume valuable resources and energy.

Unfit	Fit	Healthy
not insulated nor sealed against air leakage	normally insulated walls, properly caulked and sealed	highly insulated, airtight walls (R-2000)
single-glazed windows, no weatherstripping	double-pane windows with good weatherstripping	high-performance windows (triple-pane or low-E glass)
loose fitting, uninsulated doors, no storm doors	tight-fitting doors with good weatherstripping	insulated doors with high-quality weatherstripping
deteriorated or damaged exterior finishes, visible damage	exterior finishes in good condition, but may require high maintenance	durable, low-maintenance exterior finishes

Attics and roofs

Some attics have the potential to be converted into high quality living space suitable for bedrooms or a home office. The premature replacement of roof coverings, such as asphalt shingles, represents a waste of resources, and in some areas, an avoidable burden on landfill sites. Attics and roofs often represent an opportunity to add insulation and upgrade attic ventilation cost effectively.

Unfit	Fit	Healthy
little or no attic/roof insulation	minimum level of insulation required by codes	high level of attic and roof insulation over entire area and an effective air barrier
evidence of water damage, mold and musty smell	dry attic/roof with good natural ventilation	dry, naturally ventilated attic and roof with high and low vents
sagging/rotting roof or ceiling members	dry, sound attic/roof structure with minimal insulation	dry, sound attic/roof structure with all penetrations properly sealed
no useable attic space	attic convertible to future living space	attic properly insulated and finished for use as living space
deteriorated roofing material	conventional roofing material in good condition	durable roofing material in good condition

Termites and other pests

Infestation of a wood-frame house by termites is a serious problem that can lead to dangerous structural damage. Other pests can introduce disease into a house, and damage electrical wiring which may cause a fire.

Unfit	Fit	Healthy
termite infestation	no termites	protection against termites provided or house located in termite-free zone
birds in roof/attic or chimney	no nesting birds	proper screens and barriers to birds
rodent infestation (mice, chipmunks, squirrels, rats)	no rodents	all penetration in house properly sealed—rodent barriers installed
insect infestation	no insects	all penetration in house properly sealed
raccoons living in house	no raccoons	secure barriers to raccoons installed

Security

The safety and security of the occupants in a house can be improved through appropriate sensors, alarms, security lighting and secure hardware.. For the elderly, proper handrails on stairs and grab bars in washrooms are important security features along with anti-scald bath and shower taps. A Healthy House offers superior security outdoors and indoors.

Unfit	Fit	Healthy
no smoke alarms	regularly checked, smoke alarms in basement and on every floor	smoke alarms in basement and on every floor, carbon monoxide (CO) alarm in houses with wood heating
no outside lighting	outside lighting with manual switch	outside lighting, motion or timer controlled
no light switch at top and bottom of stairs	light switches according to minimum code requirements	lowered light switches arranged so occupants are never in the dark, or with motion sensors
no security hardware on windows and doors	minimum required security hardware	high-quality security hardware and burglar alarm
no door viewer	door viewer provided	door viewer and intercom or closed circuit camera
missing or loose handrails or guards on stairs	handrails and guards as per minimum code requirements	easy-to-grasp handrails and secure guards on both sides of stairs
no grab bars in washroom	grab bars in tub and shower	provision of grab bars, non-slip surfaces and accessible washroom

Landscaping

Watering lawns and gardens has caused water shortages in cities and rural areas. Healthy landscapes minimize the need for watering and maintenance, and avoid the growth of weeds and plants that cause allergies.

Unfit	Fit	Healthy
site drainage inadequate, directing water runoff towards the building	properly graded site	grading and landscaping, or collection device, detain water runoff and minimize load on storm water management system
mosquito breeding grounds on or near property	no or few mosquitoes	insect repelling plants and natural insect predators
large lawn area in places with water shortages	sufficient lawn area for play and recreation	low-growth native ground cover with underground watering system
no sidewalks or walkways for safe, year-round access to dwelling	acceptable sidewalks and walkways	fully barrier-free house—interior and exterior
unkept landscape fostering allergy-causing weeds	well maintained landscape	pesticide-free landscape combined with garden for vegetables, fruit and herbs
no trees	trees and shrubs	trees and shrubs provide shading of house in summer and protection against wind in winter

CMHC Publications

The following publications offer more information on the topics described in this section. To order publications, visit our website at www.cmhc.ca or call 1-800-668-2642. The publication order numbers are shown in the brackets below.

Building Materials for the Environmentally Hypersensitive (61089)

Cleaning up Your House After a Flood (61094)

Clean-up Procedures for Mold in Houses (61091)

Healthy Housing™ Renovation Planner (60957)

Investigating, Diagnosing and Treating Your Damp Basement (61065)

The Clean Air Guide: How to Identify and Correct Indoor Air Problems in Your Home (61082)

Renovator's Technical Guide (61946)

Lead in Your Home (61941)

CHAPTER ELEVEN

MAINTENANCE CALENDAR

HOMEOWNER'S MAINTENANCE CALENDAR

A house needs a lot of tender loving care, but we tend to let it go until it demands attention because it has become ugly, uncomfortable or even dangerous. This calendar is a weekly guide to help you take care of all the routine tasks around your home. Everything is listed at its right time so you won't forget anything during the year. Whole house maintenance is much less intimidating when it is planned out in small pieces.

Simply make a quick inspection of each item that applies to your house the week that it is listed here and check it off so that you will know it has been examined.

A well-kept maintenance checklist, such as this, will give you a valuable maintenance history of your house, which can help when it comes time to sell. A house with a complete and clear maintenance history removes a buyer's fears of hidden or impending trouble.

A house is always changing. Inspection and maintenance is a continuous task which will protect your investment and assure your family's safety and comfort. A few minutes every week can be the best investment you ever make.

January

Week one

FILTERS

- ❏ Forced air furnace—clean or replace, if dirty.
- ❏ Range hood—clean, if necessary.

OIL FURNACE

- ❏ Assure that barometric damper in flue pipe is functioning

Week two

FORCED AIR FURNACE

- ❏ Examine floor registers for oily dust, indicating furnace problems

ROOF

- ❏ Check for ice dams or icicles—clear roof and locate areas prone to heat loss causing snow to melt

Week three

MOISTURE DAMAGE

- ❏ Inspect kitchen, bathrooms and laundry room—stop source of moisture and repair damage.

Week four

ATTIC

- ❏ Check for frost accumulation—if any, find air leak from house and seal it. Improve attic ventilation.

February

Week one

FILTERS

- ❏ Forced air furnace—clean or replace, if dirty.
- ❏ Range hood—clean, if necessary.

Week two

SAFETY

- ❏ Repair any damaged floor coverings or steps which could be a safety hazard.
- ❏ Check security of all guards and handrails.

Week three

DRAINS

- ❏ Examine dishwasher and clear drain.
- ❏ Clean out bathtub drain.

ALARMS

- ❏ Test all fire, smoke, carbon monoxide and security alarms.

Week four

DOORS

- ❏ Oil all hinges and tighten screws as needed.

March

Week one

FILTERS

- ❏ Forced air furnace—clean or replace, if dirty.
- ❏ Range hood—clean, if necessary.

Week two

REFRIGERATORS

- ❏ Vacuum radiator grills on back of both refrigerators and freezers. Clean drip trays.

Week three

HOT WATER TANK

- ❏ Drain off a dishpan full of water from hot water tank clean-out valve (at bottom of tank) in order to control sediment and maintain efficiency.

Week four

DRIVEWAYS and WALKWAYS

- ❏ Check for frost damage.

April

Week one

EAVESTROUGHS and DOWNSPOUTS

- ❏ Check for secure attachment to house, loose joints.
- ❏ Clear obstructions.
- ❏ Assure water discharges away from foundation or into a dry well.

CAULKING

- ❏ Check all outdoor caulking at windows, doors, other penetrations.

FILTERS

- ❏ Range hood—clean if necessary.

Week two

ATTIC

- ❏ Inspect ventilation for birds' nests in vents; insulation covering soffit vents.
- ❏ Look carefully for signs of water leakage from roof.

Week three

LANDSCAPING

- ❏ Inspect grading of property around house to keep water away from foundation: raise low flower beds; divert run off from hills; improve drainage for window wells that do not drain.
- ❏ Ensure water from downspouts does not pool near the foundation wall.

Week four

SIDING

- ❏ Examine for water penetration and need for cleaning or painting.

STORMS and SCREENS

- ❏ Remove storm windows and store for the season.
- ❏ Bring screen doors and window screens out of winter storage and install. Replace screen or repair holes.

May

Week one
FOUNDATIONS
- ❏ Examine foundation walls for cracks, leaks and moisture.

Week two
FENCES
- ❏ Repair or paint fences.

HUMIDIFIERS
- ❏ Shut down and clean furnace humidifier.
- ❏ Close furnace humidifier damper on units with central air conditioning.

GAS FURNACE
- ❏ Turn OFF gas furnace and fireplace pilot lights where possible.

Week three
WATER
- ❏ Have well water tested for quality.

INSECTS
- ❏ Check all wood near soil for insect damage.

ALARMS
- ❏ Test all fire, smoke, carbon monoxide and security alarms.

Week four
FILTERS
- ❏ Range hood—clean, if necessary.
- ❏ Air conditioners—clean or replace, if dirty.
- ❏ Ventilation system—wash or replace.

June

Week one
SEPTIC TANK
- ❏ Measure sludge and scum to determine if it needs to be emptied—usually every three years.

CARPETS
- ❏ Deep clean carpets and rugs once a year.

Week two
WOOD HEATING
- ❏ Sweep chimney connected to any wood burning appliance or fireplace and inspect for end of season problems.

CLOTHES DRYER
- ❏ Vacuum lint from ducts and areas surrounding the clothes dryer.

Week three
ROOF
- ❏ Check general condition of roof—climb up or use binoculars.
- ❏ Note any sagging that could indicate structural problems to be further investigated inside the attic.
- ❏ Note the condition of all shingles—repair or replacement.
- ❏ Examine all roof flashings (for example, chimney and roof joints) as these are the primary points of leakage.

Week four
DRIVEWAY
- ❏ Repair or resurface, as needed.

FILTERS
- ❏ Range hood—clean, if necessary.
- ❏ Air conditioners—clean or replace, if dirty.

July

Week one
FAUCETS
- ❏ Change all faucet washers in the house which do not close completely and cause dripping. Washers that need frequent replacement may indicate the need for faucet repair.

Week two
FUSES
- ❏ Inspect fuse box for oversized fuses. These are signs of problems with the electrical distribution system.

Week three
SECURITY
- ❏ Check security against break-ins: lights and visibility around outside of house; quality and condition of catches and locks; verify that every possible entrance is protected; verify that the whole family has good security habits.

Week four
FILTERS
- ❏ Range hood—clean, if necessary.
- ❏ Air conditioners—clean or replace, if dirty.

August

Week one
POWER LINES
- ❏ Visually inspect electrical service lines for secure attachment where they enter the house. Check for water leakage into house along electrical conduit.

Week two
CONDENSATION
- ❏ Check basement cold water pipes for condensation and dripping.

GARAGE
- ❏ Inspect and lubricate garage door mechanism.

Week three
DOORS
- ❏ Examine all doors for binding or poor latching.

FILTERS
- ❏ Range hood—clean if necessary.
- ❏ Air conditioners—clean or replace, if dirty.
- ❏ Ventilation system—wash or replace.

ALARMS
- ❏ Test all fire, smoke, carbon monoxide and security alarms.

Week four
WINDOWS
- ❏ Check smooth mechanical functioning of all windows and lubricate where appropriate.
- ❏ Inspect window putty on outside of glass panes.
- ❏ Upgrade weatherstripping and indoor caulking.
- ❏ Repaint window frames as necessary—before the weather gets cold.

September

Week one
SIDING
- ❏ Examine house siding for water penetration or need for cleaning or painting.

Week two
HEATING
- ❏ Book annual professional tune-up for oil furnace or boiler. (Gas every two years)
- ❏ Check condition of all flue pipes and chimneys.
- ❏ Inspect oil tank for leaks.
- ❏ Inspect for water leaks in hot water or steam heating systems.
- ❏ Lubricate circulating pump on hot water heating systems.

- ❏ Turn ON gas furnace pilot light.

- ❏ Open furnace humidifier damper on units with central air conditioning. Clean humidifier.

Week three
BASEBOARD HEATERS
- ❏ Vacuum elements of baseboard electric heaters before the first use for heating season to avoid "cooking" the summer's dust.

Week four
HOT WATER RADIATORS
- ❏ Bleed air from hot water radiators.

WOOD HEATING
- ❏ Inspect chimney for wood burning appliance or fireplace for obstructions and loose joints before the heating season. Sweep clean if necessary.

October

Week one
FILTERS
- ❏ Forced air furnace—clean or replace, if dirty.
- ❏ Range hood—clean, if necessary.

NOISY FURNACE FAN
- ❏ Examine forced air furnace fan belt for wear, looseness or noise.
- ❏ Examine fan blades for dirt build-up and carefully clean if necessary. (Don't forget to disconnect the electricity to the fan motor.)

COLD AIR DRAFTS
- ❏ Inspect and upgrade weatherstripping and caulking on the inside of the house.

Week two
PROTECTION FROM FREEZING
- ❏ Drain outdoor hose bibs.
- ❏ Cover outside of air conditioners.

SCREENS and STORM WINDOWS
- ❏ Remove screen doors and store for the winter.

- ❏ Remove screens from the inside of casement windows to allow air from the heating system to keep condensation off window glass.
- ❏ Remove screens from other windows and store for the winter.
- ❏ Install winter storm windows.

Week three
SEPTIC TANK
- ❏ Measure sludge and scum to determine if it needs to be emptied before the spring.

LANDSCAPING
- ❏ Erect snow fences.
- ❏ Prepare plants for winter.

Week four
EAVESTROUGHS and DRAINS
- ❏ Clean leaves from eavestroughs and flat top roofs.
- ❏ Inspect joints and discharge from eavestroughs.

November

Week one
FILTERS
- ❏ Forced air furnace—clean or replace, if dirty.
- ❏ Range hood—clean, if necessary.

Week two
BASEBOARD HEATERS
- ❏ Check for over-heating of furniture and drapes near baseboard electric heaters.

EXHAUST FANS
- ❏ Verify that air in fact comes out of the outdoor rain hoods. Many fans make noise but don't move air.

Week three
ALARMS
- ❏ Test all fire, smoke, carbon monoxide and security alarms.
- ❏ Vacuum out all fire and smoke detectors (dust or spider webs can prevent them from functioning).

Week four
HOUSE STRUCTURE
- ❏ Note any CHANGE in sagging, springy or warped floors—this could indicate structural problems.
- ❏ Inspect structural framework of the basement for sagging or rot.

December

Week one
FILTERS
- ❏ Forced air furnace—clean or replace, if dirty.
- ❏ Range hood—clean, if necessary.

FIRE EXTINGUISHERS
- ❏ Verify that extinguishers are charged and operational.

Week two
ELECTRICAL SAFETY
- ❏ Study extension cord use throughout the house. The constant use of extension cords indicates the need for new safely-installed outlets.

Week three
HAPPY HOLIDAYS
- ❏ Check the fire safety of your Christmas lights. Plugs and wires should not be warm to the touch.

Week four
ICE PROBLEMS
- ❏ Examine windows and doors for ice accumulation which may indicate a lack of insulation or cold air leaks which should be sealed.

CONDENSATION ON WINDOWS
- ❏ Reduce sources of humidity and use exhaust fans to increase household ventilation.

HEALTHY HOUSING ™ MAINTENANCE CALENDAR

January

Week one

FILTERS

- ❏ Forced air furnace—clean or replace, if dirty.
- ❏ Range hood—clean, if necessary.

OIL FURNACE

- ❏ Assure that barometric damper in flue pipe is functioning

Week two

FORCED AIR FURNACE

- ❏ Examine floor registers for oily dust, indicating furnace problems

ROOF

- ❏ Check for ice dams or icicles—clear roof and locate areas prone to heat loss causing snow to melt

Week three

MOISTURE DAMAGE

- ❏ Inspect kitchen, bathrooms and laundry room—stop source of moisture and repair damage.

Week four

ATTIC

- ❏ Check for frost accumulation—if any, find air leak from house and seal it. Improve attic ventilation.

February

Week one

FILTERS

- ❏ Forced air furnace—clean or replace, if dirty.
- ❏ Range hood—clean, if necessary.

Week two

SAFETY

- ❏ Repair any damaged floor coverings or steps which could be a safety hazard.
- ❏ Check security of all guards and handrails.

Week three

DRAINS

- ❏ Examine dishwasher and clear drain.
- ❏ Clean out bathtub drain.

ALARMS

- ❏ Test all fire, smoke, carbon monoxide and security alarms.

Week four

DOORS

- ❏ Oil all hinges and tighten screws as needed.

March

Week one

FILTERS

- ❏ Forced air furnace—clean or replace, if dirty.
- ❏ Range hood—clean, if necessary.

Week two

REFRIGERATORS

- ❏ Vacuum radiator grills on back of both refrigerators and freezers. Clean drip trays.

Week three

HOT WATER TANK

- ❏ Drain off a dishpan full of water from hot water tank clean-out valve (at bottom of tank) in order to control sediment and maintain efficiency.

Week four

DRIVEWAYS and WALKWAYS

- ❏ Check for frost damage.

April

Week one

EAVESTROUGHS and DOWNSPOUTS

- ❏ Check for secure attachment to house, loose joints.
- ❏ Clear obstructions.
- ❏ Assure water discharges away from foundation or into a dry well.

CAULKING

- ❏ Check all outdoor caulking at windows, doors, other penetrations.

FILTERS

- ❏ Range hood—clean if necessary.

Week two

ATTIC

- ❏ Inspect ventilation for birds' nests in vents; insulation covering soffit vents.
- ❏ Look carefully for signs of water leakage from roof.

Week three

LANDSCAPING

- ❏ Inspect grading of property around house to keep water away from foundation: raise low flower beds; divert run off from hills; improve drainage for window wells that do not drain.
- ❏ Ensure water from downspouts does not pool near the foundation wall.

Week four

SIDING

- ❏ Examine for water penetration and need for cleaning or painting.

STORMS and SCREENS

- ❏ Remove storm windows and store for the season.
- ❏ Bring screen doors and window screens out of winter storage and install. Replace screen or repair holes.

May

Week one

FOUNDATIONS

- ❏ Examine foundation walls for cracks, leaks and moisture.

Week two

FENCES

- ❏ Repair or paint fences.

HUMIDIFIERS

- ❏ Shut down and clean furnace humidifier.
- ❏ Close furnace humidifier damper on units with central air conditioning.

GAS FURNACE

- ❏ Turn OFF gas furnace and fireplace pilot lights where possible.

Week three

WATER

- ❏ Have well water tested for quality.

INSECTS

- ❏ Check all wood near soil for insect damage.

ALARMS

- ❏ Test all fire, smoke, carbon monoxide and security alarms.

Week four

FILTERS

- ❏ Range hood—clean, if necessary.
- ❏ Air conditioners—clean or replace, if dirty.
- ❏ Ventilation system—wash or replace.

June

Week one

SEPTIC TANK

- ❏ Measure sludge and scum to determine if it needs to be emptied—usually every three years.

CARPETS

- ❏ Deep clean carpets and rugs once a year.

Week two

WOOD HEATING

- ❏ Sweep chimney connected to any wood burning appliance or fireplace and inspect for end of season problems.

CLOTHES DRYER

- ❏ Vacuum lint from ducts and areas surrounding the clothes dryer.

Week three

ROOF

- ❏ Check general condition of roof—climb up or use binoculars.
- ❏ Note any sagging that could indicate structural problems to be further investigated inside the attic.
- ❏ Note the condition of all shingles—repair or replacement.
- ❏ Examine all roof flashings (for example, chimney and roof joints) as these are the primary points of leakage.

Week four

DRIVEWAY

- ❏ Repair or resurface, as needed.

FILTERS

- ❏ Range hood—clean, if necessary.
- ❏ Air conditioners—clean or replace, if dirty.

July

Week one
FAUCETS

❏ Change all faucet washers in the house which do not close completely and cause dripping. Washers that need frequent replacement may indicate the need for faucet repair.

Week two
FUSES

❏ Inspect fuse box for over-sized fuses. These are signs of problems with the electrical distribution system.

Week three
SECURITY

❏ Check security against break-ins: lights and visibility around outside of house; quality and condition of catches and locks; verify that every possible entrance is protected; verify that the whole family has good security habits.

Week four
FILTERS

❏ Range hood—clean, if necessary.

❏ Air conditioners—clean or replace, if dirty.

August

Week one
POWER LINES

❏ Visually inspect electrical service lines for secure attachment where they enter the house. Check for water leakage into house along electrical conduit.

Week two
CONDENSATION

❏ Check basement cold water pipes for condensation and dripping.

GARAGE

❏ Inspect and lubricate garage door mechanism.

Week three
DOORS

❏ Examine all doors for binding or poor latching.

FILTERS

❏ Range hood—clean if necessary.

❏ Air conditioners—clean or replace, if dirty.

❏ Ventilation system—wash or replace.

ALARMS

❏ Test all fire, smoke, carbon monoxide and security alarms.

Week four
WINDOWS

❏ Check smooth mechanical functioning of all windows and lubricate where appropriate.

❏ Inspect window putty on outside of glass panes.

❏ Upgrade weatherstripping and indoor caulking.

❏ Repaint window frames as necessary—before the weather gets cold.

September

Week one
SIDING

❏ Examine house siding for water penetration or need for cleaning or painting.

Week two
HEATING

❏ Book annual professional tune-up for oil furnace or boiler. (Gas every two years)

❏ Check condition of all flue pipes and chimneys.

❏ Inspect oil tank for leaks.

❏ Inspect for water leaks in hot water or steam heating systems.

❏ Lubricate circulating pump on hot water heating systems.

❏ Turn ON gas furnace pilot light.

❏ Open furnace humidifier damper on units with central air conditioning. Clean humidifier.

Week three
BASEBOARD HEATERS

❏ Vacuum elements of baseboard electric heaters before the first use for heating season to avoid "cooking" the summer's dust.

Week four
HOT WATER RADIATORS

❏ Bleed air from hot water radiators.

WOOD HEATING

❏ Inspect chimney for wood burning appliance or fireplace for obstructions and loose joints before the heating season. Sweep clean if necessary.

October

Week one
FILTERS

❏ Forced air furnace—clean or replace, if dirty.

❏ Range hood—clean, if necessary.

NOISY FURNACE FAN

❏ Examine forced air furnace fan belt for wear, looseness or noise.

❏ Examine fan blades for dirt build-up and carefully clean if necessary. (Don't forget to disconnect the electricity to the fan motor.)

COLD AIR DRAFTS

❏ Inspect and upgrade weatherstripping and caulking on the inside of the house.

Week two
PROTECTION FROM FREEZING

❏ Drain outdoor hose bibs.

❏ Cover outside of air conditioners.

SCREENS and STORM WINDOWS

❏ Remove screen doors and store for the winter.

❏ Remove screens from the inside of casement windows to allow air from the heating system to keep condensation off window glass.

❏ Remove screens from other windows and store for the winter.

❏ Install winter storm windows.

Week three
SEPTIC TANK

❏ Measure sludge and scum to determine if it needs to be emptied before the spring.

LANDSCAPING

❏ Erect snow fences.

❏ Prepare plants for winter.

Week four
EAVESTROUGHS and DRAINS

❏ Clean leaves from eavestroughs and flat top roofs.

❏ Inspect joints and discharge from eavestroughs.

November

Week one
FILTERS

❏ Forced air furnace—clean or replace, if dirty.

❏ Range hood—clean, if necessary.

Week two
BASEBOARD HEATERS

❏ Check for over-heating of furniture and drapes near baseboard electric heaters.

EXHAUST FANS

❏ Verify that air in fact comes out of the outdoor rain hoods. Many fans make noise but don't move air.

Week three
ALARMS

❏ Test all fire, smoke, carbon monoxide and security alarms.

❏ Vacuum out all fire and smoke detectors (dust or spider webs can prevent them from functioning).

Week four
HOUSE STRUCTURE

❏ Note any CHANGE in sagging, springy or warped floors—this could indicate structural problems.

❏ Inspect structural framework of the basement for sagging or rot.

December

Week one
FILTERS

❏ Forced air furnace—clean or replace, if dirty.

❏ Range hood—clean, if necessary.

FIRE EXTINGUISHERS

❏ Verify that extinguishers are charged and operational.

Week two
ELECTRICAL SAFETY

❏ Study extension cord use throughout the house. The constant use of extension cords indicates the need for new safely-installed outlets.

Week three
HAPPY HOLIDAYS

❏ Check the fire safety of your Christmas lights. Plugs and wires should not be warm to the touch.

Week four
ICE PROBLEMS

❏ Examine windows and doors for ice accumulation which may indicate a lack of insulation or cold air leaks which should be sealed.

CONDENSATION ON WINDOWS

❏ Reduce sources of humidity and use exhaust fans to increase household ventilation.